REMINISCENCES OF A MUSICIAN

THE HOUSEBOAT ON THE DANUBE

REMINISCENCES OF A MUSICIAN

By Clayton Johns

CAMBRIDGE

WASHBURN & THOMAS

1929

TO
MY UNPROFESSIONAL FRIEND
HENRY MCKEAN INGERSOLL

A WORD IN ADVANCE

THE events recorded in these pages cover, for the most part, a period of forty-six years — from 1882 to 1928. During that time the world has entirely changed, music and everything else. In 1882 there were no automobiles, no airplanes, and no telephones. For the sake of music, I went to Berlin. After a stay of two years abroad, I returned to Boston where I have been living ever since, except for frequent trips to Europe. The following "notes" of this simple tale are recorded *on* and *between* the lines of the musical staff. Those *above* and *below* the staff, unrecorded, may be left to the imagination.

C. J.

Brimmer Chambers
January, 1929

ILLUSTRATIONS

REMINISCENCES OF A MUSICIAN

MY first American ancestor, Richard Johns "of the Cliffs," Maryland, came from Carmarthenshire, Wales, in 1692. His great-grandson (my great-grandfather Kensey Johns of Sudley, West River, Maryland) came to New Castle, Delaware, to read law with George Read, one of the signers of the Declaration of Independence. In direct line from Richard Johns of the Cliffs through Kensey Johns of Sudley, I was born on the twenty-fourth day of November, 1857, in New Castle on the Delaware River, a little below Mason and Dixon's line. Unlike Topsy, New Castle never "growed" before or after my time. It was then, as it still is, a quaint, old-fashioned town with a population of about two thousand. There were no factories and there was no business. It was said that the inhabitants could not bear the sound of a hammer.

New Castle was the county seat. The courts were there. The old houses were of red brick, with gardens, something like the Salem houses in Massachusetts. Along the river and on one side of the town was a "Battery" with trees and benches which formed a promenade where the beaux and belles disported themselves. All gone, long ago, but I remember. The streets were densely shaded by old trees, as was the Village Green, around which stood the courthouse, schoolhouse, jail, and church. The tower of the church, to which Queen Anne presented the Communion service, bears the date of 1689. In the churchyard are some characteristic tombs — one of the eighteenth century. On its marble slab is sculptured a rock on which a large mother (or father) duck has got to heaven, while three ducklings are climbing up the rock, hoping to get there.

Another feature of the old town was the whipping post where criminals got their deserts. This stood in the jail yard. On either side of it were places for the hands of the criminal to be whipped. On a platform at the top of the post was the pillory where the victim, standing perhaps for an hour with head and hands confined, received an extra punishment before the whipping. The number of lashes with cat-o'-nine-tails varied, being sometimes thirty, sometimes forty or more on the bare back — often drawing blood. The authorities of Delaware maintained that the whipping post was a deterrent to crime; it was also commonly believed that an offender was never brought to punishment a second time. Some years ago the courthouse, jail, and whipping post were removed to Wilmington.

Reverting to the courts and the judiciary: only a few of the States had a chancellor. Delaware was one. The chancellorship, coming down from old English tradition, was the highest judicial office, the chancellor ranking above the chief justice. Many of the good people of New Castle were either judicial or ecclesiastical. The society, therefore, was cultivated

5

and genial. (There was a bookish library at one end of the Village Green, near the church.) In later years the town began to lose its distinction; the old people died while the young people sought a more active life elsewhere; so, like Ichabod's, its "glory has departed."

In New Castle I lived for eighteen years. In spite of the natural pressure of tradition, I refused to study law, nor did I ever think of becoming a parson. My own wish was to study music, but, as one of my elders said: "Clayton, I don't want you to be a fiddler or a dancing master," and so a compromise was made in favor of architecture, which I pursued for three years in the office of Mr Theophilus P. Chandler in Philadelphia.

Then, being of age, I followed my strong desire, going to Harvard where for two years I studied composition with John Knowles Paine and the piano with William H. Sherwood. At the end of this time, I moved from Cambridge to Boston where

6

SOME OF THE OLD NEW CASTLE HOUSES. I

THE house of my great-great-grandfather, Nicholas Van Dyke, Governor of Delaware, at that time called "President of the State." His daughter Nancy married my great-grandfather Kensey Johns, Chancellor of Delaware. Washington came to the wedding and kissed the bride, or, as a chronicle says:"Framing the bride's face between his hands and gently kissing her on the forehead." Another chronicle says that ten years later, when Washington and my ancestor met again, Washington said: "You must be a happy man, Mr Johns, to have such a beautiful wife."

I lived for one year more, continuing my study with Sherwood.

John Knowles Paine, in those days — 1881 — was the leading American composer. He was at the head of the music department of Harvard University. His "First" and his "Spring" symphonies were performed by Theodore Thomas's orchestra on tour. His music for "Œdipus Tyrannus" was produced under the auspices of the classical department of the University. Mr Paine was a genial companion with a keen sense of humor. Having been teacher and pupil, we became good, I may say intimate, friends.

ON JUNE 28, 1882, I sailed in the good ship *Scythia*, at that time one of the foremost Cunarders. She was rated at nearly five thousand tons; the great liners now register more than fifty. The *Scythia* had only one deck on which we lived and had our being. Everything happened on this deck. The chairs were placed in rows, and those in the back row were roped to an

7

iron rail in order to prevent their sliding down to the scuppers. Often there was a general spill occasioned by an unexpected higher wave. There was no wooden covering over the deck — only an awning rolled back when it didn't rain. When it *did* rain, the awning was very leaky. Shuffleboard and other sports took place on the one deck, where also the unwell passengers sat and took their meals. The only other resort, excepting a small smoking room, was the saloon where we were fed and where we played games and made music. There was an upright piano at one end of the saloon. The piano was in frequent use whether we liked music or not. Supper, at about ten o'clock, was a pleasant occasion. Little groups of passengers sat about, chatting, eating grilled bones and sardines, and drinking lemonade.

As I had never crossed the ocean before, everything was new and interesting to me. A flying fish came on board and was caught by one of the sailors. Then there were whales spouting, and possibly there was an iceberg. (On subsequent trips I saw icebergs by the dozen — fortunately not "on speaking terms".) The trip lasted for ten days.

A pilot boat, in those days, was a little schooner of private ownership carrying two or three pilots. A number of such pilot boats, each hoping to pick up the first incoming steamer, sailed off shore, often for several hundred miles, beating about in all sorts of weather. When a pilot boat succeeded in picking up a steamer, the pilot, wearing a silk hat (!), climbed up the side of the ship, bringing with him a roll of newspapers, usually several days old. The pilot then took the ship in charge, while the captain and the other officers gave him a warm welcome and something else. The various pilot boats were scattered over the sea like birds of prey. They were distinguished by large numerals on their sails, easily to be seen at quite a distance. This gave a chance to sporting passengers to form a pool as they neared port, betting on which pilot's number would turn up first. Pilots now belong to a "company," so there is no competition. The pilot goes out a few miles beyond quarantine, just far enough to meet the incoming steamer.

After a happy voyage we landed in Liverpool at about ten o'clock in the evening, in broad daylight. As "daylight saving" had not then been invented, the English natural daylight made us feel queer. By the time we had reached the Adelphi Hotel, the streets were brilliantly lighted. The friends with whom I was traveling had engaged a courier in advance. When we arrived at the hotel, the corridors were a blaze of light. Rows of servants standing, bowing and scraping, unaccustomed to our simple American ways, annoyed us and at the same time amused us. We felt sure that the manager of the hotel must have thought he had caught a real American goldfish. The next morning we breakfasted on fried sole, English muffins, and Dundee marmalade — all delicious. The sole was real sole; the muffins were real

SOME OF THE OLD NEW CASTLE HOUSES. II

THE house of my great-grandfather Kensey Johns, Chancellor
of Delaware, and his wife, Nancy Van Dyke Johns.

English muffins; and the real marmalade came from Dundee. Nowadays we have all these things at home — excepting sole, which does not swim in our waters.

From Liverpool we went to Chester, getting our first thrill of antiquity: the Cathedral, the Wall, King Charles's Tower, the quaint old houses, and all the rest of it. My literary traveling companion, J. W. S., was a Wordsworthian, and we steeped ourselves in Wordsworthian poetry, meaning to tramp through the Lake Country and to stop at all the various places mentioned by the poet. As a fact, owing to the frequent showers which occurred that summer and, indeed, recur every summer among the Lakes, we drove most of the time. At Hawkeshead, where Wordsworth studied in his youth, a youngster showed us the desk on which Wordsworth's name was carved. As the boy said: "It must have been done by him, because in those days every lad carved his name on his desk." Rain or shine, the landscape was lovely, and we pursued our way with de-

light as far as Ullswater, where we spent
a Sunday and where I met Mr Edward
Hecht, an English musician of whom I
shall have more to say at another time.

It is not my purpose to emulate Mark
Twain's "Innocents Abroad." Let me
briefly say that we traveled along the
west coast of England, stopping at interesting places, as far as the Scotch lakes,
then to Edinburgh and down along the
east coast, stopping at abbeys, cathedrals,
universities, and finally arriving in London. Here we remained for a fortnight and
here I got another thrill from seeing the
Old Masters in the National Gallery.

AFTER crossing the channel and going
through Belgium, we went up the Rhine
to Frankfort, Heidelberg, and Nuremberg — the gateway to Bayreuth. Traveling with an unprofessional musical friend,
we stopped for the night at Nuremberg.
The crowd going and coming was so great
that Owen Wister, returning from the performance of *Parsifal*, could not get a room

in the hotel, so we took him into our double room. Out of the kindness of his heart my unprofessional friend offered his bed to Wister and slept in the bathroom while Wister and I talked most of the night. Wister told me of an amusing incident which had happened in the train. Wister, explaining the characters in the play to some one in the carriage, said: "Gurnemanz is a tiresome old chappie who makes long speeches." Thereupon a German cried out: "Oh, he is a knight of zee Grail!" That was sufficient to satisfy "a perfect Wagnerite." (By the way, isn't it true that there is at least *one* tiresome old chappie in every Wagner opera because the old chappie has to put the story together?) True or not — after a night in Nuremberg we went to see and hear for ourselves.

Having arrived in Bayreuth, we climbed the hill to the theatre, feeling like pilgrims approaching Mecca. *Parsifal* was being performed for the first time that summer. Liszt and Wagner were walking about in

the corridors between the acts, and outside of the theatre. Winckelmann was
the Parsifal; Materna, the Kundry; and
the conductor of the whole was Hans
Richter. Before the performance began,
the trumpet theme was blown from the
outside gallery. (I am told the same effect
is nowadays produced at the Bach Festival in Bethlehem, when a chorale is played
by trumpets from a church tower.) The
sound of the first notes of the Prelude, rising out of the darkness of the Bayreuth
theatre, made an impression on me never
to be forgotten. I have heard it many
times since, but never to equal my first
performance.

Hans Richter was the greatest of all
orchestral leaders, not only for Wagner's
operas, but for symphonic music. Richter's
concerts in London were an annual insti-
tution. I often heard them there. I always
felt that no matter what was played, it
sounded right. Richter's conducting was
like stroking the fur of a cat the right
way, never rubbing it up the wrong way.

SOME OF THE OLD NEW CASTLE HOUSES. III

My grandfather's (Kensey Johns, Jr) and my father's house, in which I was born and where I lived for eighteen years. This was across the garden from my great-grandfather's house. Diagonally opposite to it was the house of my great-great-uncle, Nicholas Van Dyke, Jr, United States Senator. His daughter married Charles Irenée du Pont. Lafayette stayed here and came to the wedding. The chair in which he sat is highly prized by one of my Van Dyke-du Pont cousins.

Richter, like Joachim, had a very big head and body. Both men had many offers to come to America, but both always refused. Joachim feared the sea. Richter, perhaps, had "so many children he didn't know what to do." I once saw a whole row of his young ones walking in single file. Some one told me they were numbered because their father couldn't remember all their names.

After having left Bayreuth, we went to Munich, passing several days there, getting another taste of beautiful pictures and of good Munich beer. As Salzburg was not far from Munich, we spent a day or two *there*, seeing for the first time a snow mountain. Salzburg is filled with Mozart memories, to which I duly paid tribute. Since the salt mines were within driving distance, we went to see them. Rigged out in the most unsightly costumes, each of us holding a candle, we entered a hole in the ground. The guide placed us in a row on an inclined slide of wood, smooth as glass. On the right of the slide was a rope which we grasped with our right hands, protected by pieces of leather. The guide, being the last man holding back the others, suddenly gave a signal and let go. We plunged downwards like greased lightning. The candles, of course, went out promptly. Down, down, downer — we were left in complete darkness, until we were held up stock-still at the bottom of the slide. Having made the first descent, we crossed a lake as gruesome as the infernal regions. Passing through more galleries and by caverns, we began to ascend. Having reached the highest point, we were mounted on a double-runner with wheels. The guide cried out, "Let go!" and once more, again it seemed for miles, we were shot with lightning speed into daylight. We then had ourselves photographed in our droll costumes.

After having spent the morning in the bowels of the earth, we spent the afternoon going up to the end of the Königsee, that lovely lake. It was Sunday. The peasants were wearing their best Tyrolean costumes, dancing, and singing their best songs, forming a picturesque foreground, while the lake and snow mountains made a beautiful background.

Our next stop was in Vienna, where we remained for some days. The opera was "going." Materna and the great singers were singing. Edouard Strauss was conducting his band at the Volksgarten. We went to the races in the Prater and spent some time at the picture gallery. At the end of my stay, I went to the cemetery to visit Beethoven's and Schubert's graves and picked some ivy leaves which I still preserve. The next day I left Vienna for Berlin. My summer holiday was over. After a few days at the hotel, I found lodgings for the winter.

MR HECHT, whom I had met in the English Lakes, had given me a letter of introduction to Joachim, the great violinist. After my arrival in Berlin, Joachim received me in a very friendly way. He was naturally kind and genial. Under his in-

fluence I began to study with several
teachers belonging to the faculty of the
Hochschule. My work with them was entirely private. Friedrich Grabau, with
whom I studied the piano, was a very
musical person, a lover of the best. He
was not a great pianist — not even a
great teacher — but he led me into paths
of musical righteousness.

After I had studied with Grabau for a
year, he fell ill, and I was obliged to make
a change. The change was in favor of
Oscar Raif, with whom I continued to
study until I left Berlin in June, 1884.
Raif was a born teacher from whom I got
many valuable hints. My teacher in coun-
terpoint and composition was Friedrich
Kiel, a delightful old gentleman, I should
think something like "Papa Haydn."
When I asked Joachim about Kiel, Joachim said: "Nobody is so good as Kiel."
Kiel, like all the members of the Hochschule faculty, was violently against
Liszt and Wagner. *They* represented the
modern school, while the attitude of the

THE CHURCH AND THE LIBRARY

Usually, going to New Castle once a year, my special mission
has been to make sure that the grass has been cut and kept in
order generally for my corner of the churchyard, where the different members of my family lie at rest and where I shall join
them sooner or later, in the course of time. A year or two ago
in the church, I found a colored woman cleaning up and dust-
ing the cushions and pews. She was an "old timer" with a musical voice and gentle manner. We talked about old days. "Ah,"
said she, "everything is different now-a-days. When I was
young, there were white people, colored people, and Old Families." I then left her, wondering whether the old days hadn't a
particular charm of their own.

Hochschule was strictly classical. Kiel once said to me: "It is a sin for you to go to hear a Wagner opera." Think of that! Joachim and the others being so conservative, it was small wonder that I was blinded for a time to the greatness of Liszt and Wagner. I was young, inexperienced, and green — fresh from an America that was very different from the America of today. I can now see that "there were giants in those days." Other pianists and composers have appeared since, but the scent of the roses will still hang round Liszt and Wagner.

Let me now say a word about my daily life in Berlin in the eighties. A friend in Boston had given me a letter of introduction to Frau von Schack, a German lady of high degree who had come down in the world. She was Countess Blumenthal, niece of Field Marshal Blumenthal, and Hof-Dame (Lady-in-Waiting) to Princess Frederick Charles. As General von Schack was in waiting to Prince Frederick Charles (the "Red Prince") Countess Blumenthal and he were married in the palace under the protection of Kaiser Wilhelm and Crown Prince Frederick. All went well for some time, but unfortunately, having forged or cheated at cards or something of that sort, General von Schack was disgraced and discharged from the army. As a result, he fled to America and she with him. After two years of unhappiness in New York, she left him and returned to Berlin, determining to support herself and her two daughters. The only means of support seemed to be for her to open her house to three or four "paying guests." When I arrived at Berlin, after a few days at the hotel, I went to Frau von Schack's and stayed there for two years. My unprofessional friend of the bathroom in Nuremberg and my Wordsworthian friend of the English Lakes soon joined me to study in Berlin, and we three foregathered for the winter in the family of Frau von Schack. Frau von Schack was a delightful person and we all became great friends.

Music was my chief study, but I was

also interested in German and French. My first teacher in German was a student named Gabriel. We called him Erzengel (Archangel). He was neither angel nor archangel, but only a stupid person. By way of making conversation, I once asked him about his family. He said he had three sisters. One was "verheiratet" (married); the other two were "noch zu haben" (still to be had). Herr Gabriel took us to a "Kommers" (a students' social gathering) where the students sang songs and drank beer. Another student took us to the "Mensur" (the students' duelling place) where we watched a number of duels — students nipping off each others' ears or noses or slashing their faces. One we saw who received a gash on his cranium which caused him to flinch. That showed such a lack of pluck that he was dropped from the corps. I was interested to go once, but never again. A few years later, in Heidelberg, I saw many students who had been bandaged and plastered over their fresh wounds, parading themselves to show their bravery! The wounds were often kept open to make the scars as broad and deep as possible. I was told that the irritation of the wound was increased and the resultant scar thus made more decorative if salt and pepper were rubbed in. Many years afterwards I saw a number of bull-fights in Seville. I didn't like student duels, nor did I like bullfighting. I hardly know which I disliked the more.

To go back to my study of German: We soon dismissed the Archangel, and in his place we engaged Frau Dr Hempel with whom I studied for two years, taking lessons twice a week. Nobody ever had a better teacher. She was a wonder. She spoke English as well as German. She knew *Faust* from cover to cover. Beginning with any line she could go on to any length unprompted. She had also a delightful sense of humor. In the spring, she used to take her pupils into the country for a "Landpartie," a sort of picnic where we ate and drank and talked bad German. I still maintain she was a marvelous

22

teacher. I can't say, "Long may she live," for she died some years ago, but I *can* wish her a *requiescat*.

During the winter we went to many concerts, some good and others not so good. Also we went frequently to the theatre for the sake of improving our German. The Berlin picture gallery was representative of many different schools. Every week, Thursday afternoon, we passed an hour or two there studying the Old Masters, taking *one* room at a time each week. We also went occasionally to a lecture at the University. We were not matriculated, but certain lectures were free to the public. I remember particularly sitting under Professor Grimm who belonged to the famous Grimm family and was a delightful talker.

The weeks passed by pleasantly in Berlin. We liked everything we did. I won't say we did everything we liked. In the course of time, Christmas came along. Christmas in Germany was a great event for young and old. Frau von Schack made

Christmas merry. There was a Christmas tree, of course, and we all exchanged presents. The old countesses and the young soldier cadets belonging to the family came, so we were not made homesick in a foreign land.

After Christmas, the days being short and dull, we planned for a spring vacation. In March we set forth for a six weeks' trip to Italy, going as far as Naples. The pictures and architecture were a delight. In Rome I found some Roman-American friends who made life pleasant. Occasionally I went to a ball or went out to dine. I remember an interesting evening when Raphael's Four Hundredth Anniversary was celebrated, when Sgambati played and Prince Odescalchi spoke. The Prince's voice and his Italian were so beautiful I don't know whether his performance or Sgambati's playing pleased me the more.

We returned directly north from Rome to Venice. Venice was rather cold and windy. I like rather to think of Venice in the summer, where I passed so many happy weeks subsequently. Leaving Venice, stopping in Vienna, we returned to Berlin and our studies until July found us traveling again.

PLANNING a summer trip, I thought it would be interesting to stop at Weimar and see Liszt. I asked Joachim to give me a letter to him. He said he had seen but little of Liszt for the last ten years, as he did not like Liszt's music. Nevertheless, Joachim gave me a letter, and I went on my way rejoicing. The sequel shows whether I rejoiced or not. On July 14, 1883, with my unprofessional friend I left Berlin for Weimar. I was thinking only of *meeting* the great man, not of *playing* to him. Saturday afternoon I left my letter at the Hof-Gärtnerei, Liszt's little house in the Grand Duke's park. The servant said I might see the Meister at nine o'clock Sunday morning.

At nine o'clock I presented myself. The servant led me upstairs to the second floor. In my hand I had my hat, cane and card.

The door opened and before me stood Liszt. I tried to put my card into my trousers pocket. There I was left, full of embarrassment. Liszt said: "I see you have brought me a letter from Joachim and so forth and so forth." Then, as I fumbled about to get rid of my card, Liszt looked at my hand in my pocket and added: "Sie sind echt Amerikanisch" (You are a real American). "Oh," said I, "Wenn Sie *echt* Amerikanisch sein wollen, müssen Sie die Händen in die *beiden* Taschen stecken" (If you want to be *real* American, you must put your hands in *both* pockets). Think of my cheek! Liszt was furious, and no wonder. He said: "Wenn Sie das probiren wollen, müssen Sie weiter gehen" (If you want to try that sort of thing, you must get out). I don't think I was scared; only lacking in veneration, due perhaps to the influence of my preceptors. (In any case, I now profoundly apologized for having been such an ass.) In a few minutes Liszt recovered his temper, saying: "Probiren

Sie was *da!*" (Try something else), point-
ing to the piano.

As I have said, I hadn't the slightest
idea of playing to Liszt. My only idea was
to meet him. I did as I was bid, however,
and sat down to the piano. Then I *was*
scared. I had been studying one of the
early Beethoven Sonatas, opus 14 in G.
After I had played a few measures, Liszt
interrupted: "Das ist ein Conservatorium
Stück. Probiren Sie Etwas anders!"(That's
a Conservatory piece. Try something else).
Then I began Chopin's "Polonaise in C
minor." Liszt yanked me off the stool and
showed me how it ought to be played. I
am sorry that he played only a few measures. I remember he said that it ought to
be played "more majestically." After a
little more talk about music and musicians, he asked me to come to his house
on the following Tuesday afternoon at
four o'clock, when his pupils would play.
After the above preamble I now quote
from my old journal:

Visit to Liszt in Weimar, July 17, 1883.

Liszt lives on the second floor of the Hof-
Gärtnerei (Court Gardener's House). At
four o'clock I found about thirty young
people, of both sexes, gathered in the ves-
tibule below, waiting to be summoned by
the Master, who often sleeps in the afternoon, as Mr H. told me (Mr H. was an
old pupil of Sherwood's). Soon after I
arrived, the summons came. I went up
with the rest. Liszt stood near the door,
receiving each one as he or she entered.
By the time I had made my way in, Mr
H. was at the piano, playing a Nocturne
by Chopin. Mr H.'s playing didn't seem
to please the Master, for during the course
of the Nocturne Liszt told him four different times to go to the Conservatorium.
Presently a young woman bounced in,
Liszt calling out: "Fräulein Méloné, eine
Célébrité aus Europé," the music still
going forward. This made everybody
laugh, but it didn't disconcert Fräulein
Méloné. When Mr H. had finished the
Nocturne, Liszt said, "Und so weiter!"
(And so forth!). Liszt then called upon

28

"Essipoff die sechste" (Essipoff the sixth)
for a Chopin Concerto movement. She
began bravely, but when she fumbled a
passage, Liszt cried out, "Essipoff die
siebente" (Essipoff the seventh). The
lady recovered herself by a bold dash,
however, and Liszt said, "Essipoff die
erste" (Essipoff the first) and pulled her
from the piano stool, giving her a couple
of gentle boxes on the ear.

Next came a Miss Stevens from New
York, who seemed to be in high favor,
playing a Rubinstein* piece very nicely
until she reached the last page, when
Liszt caught her by the chin, saying,
"Gehen Sie, und lassen Sie sich photo-

---

*Let it not be forgotten that Rubinstein was
one of the stars of the first magnitude in those
days. Rubinstein and Joachim were contempo-
raries. I heard Rubinstein, the second winter I
passed in Berlin, 1883–84, from time to time.
Once, when he and Joachim played together the
Kreutzer Sonata at a private house, I sat only a
few feet behind him. I thought it was the greatest
playing I had ever heard, but Grabau, my teacher,
said afterwards that it sounded as if they had
never played it together before! Rubinstein's

graphieren!" (Go and have yourself photographed). She then sat more quietly,
kissing the old gentleman's heart when
she had finished. There was a good deal
of kissing and cheek-patting during the
afternoon.

Next came a young Fräulein who played
a Chopin Scherzo beautifully, which Liszt
seemed to like, but didn't give half the
praise he gave to others, though it was
the best playing of the afternoon. A number of others followed, more or less bad,
one particularly bad, a flibberty-gibbet
person, playing a Tarantella of Liszt's,
stumbling all the way through, getting
"Bravo, gut, und bon" *ad infinitum* from

singing touch was wonderful; with his broad fingers, he seemed able to make one tone last through
twice the usual length of time. His Barcarolles
might be mentioned as examples of his singing
quality. Rubinstein's hand was almost as broad
as it was long. His fingers were like cushions.
Often he played carelessly, but with great effect.
It was said he played so many wrong notes that he
might have made a new composition of them.
His well-known "Étude on False Notes" was
suggested, perhaps, by his carelessness.

the Master. A certain Herr Reisenauer
then played Liszt's "Auber Tarantella,"
completely annihilating all technical diffi-
culties, bringing down the house. Reisenauer has been studying with Liszt for
eight years, and has a wonderful tech-
nique. Liszt called for the "C minor Polonaise" of Chopin, saying that one of the
Herren had played it to him lately. As no
one spoke up, I became painfully con-
scious that he might be referring to me.
Mr H., who was standing near, said:
"You'd better own up, or he would get
mad." The room was searched for the
music, but it wasn't to be found. By this
time, Liszt had fixed upon me as the guilty
person. Much to my relief, he said: "Wir
wollen es das nächste Mal haben" (We
shall have it the next time). A half hour
was spent on some variations by Weitz-
mann, the theme being "Chopsticks."
Liszt made each lady who hadn't played
already take a hand, the lady playing
"Chopsticks" while Liszt played the variations. This was pretty stupid, but it

31

seemed to amuse the old gentleman and, no doubt, tickled the vanity of the ladies. After a short piece played by Fräulein Méloné, Liszt said, "Ich empfehle mich," (Good afternoon) and we all took our leave. One old lady, in doing so, kissed Liszt's hand and his heart, he kissing her pretty much all over.

The two hours I passed there were quite informal. Liszt paces up and down the room, beating time with his hands, talking to different ones who stand and sit about, leaning on the piano or tables. When anything doesn't please the old gentleman, he goes to the piano himself, playing the passage through, often mimicking the way the pupil has played it. He is fond of his joke, and equally fond of the approbation which he seeks from all sides after the explosion of his wit. I walked home with Mr H. and we compared notes about the advantages derived from a summer in Weimar with Liszt.

WHAT I have written is a verbatim account of my experience, which happened forty-five years ago. The world and music have entirely changed since then. Liszt at that time was seventy-two years old. He had long before passed his zenith. After having rested on his laurels, he went "back to the farm." His farm was Weimar, where a number of aspiring, would-be musicians were collected about him — all manner of different grades of talent and musicianship. Liszt received them all, good, bad, and indifferent, as we have seen. The hours passed after his nap on Tuesday afternoons amused him. Whether he took them seriously or not, Liszt's milk of human kindness never ceased to flow. I am speaking here only of what was called "Der Schwarm." The swarm was a hive of busy bees, coming from all parts of Europe and America, each one of them hoping to gather honey from the Master's garden. Most of Liszt's pupils who became celebrated all over the world did not belong to the swarm. The prize pupils went to the Master at other times, *not* from four to six on Tuesday afternoons. I daresay a prize pupil occasionally played in the afternoon for the swarm, capping the climax, like Reisenauer, who *did* later on make a name for himself. Whether they were the pupils of the swarm or whether it was the individual serious pupil, be it remembered that Liszt never took a penny for the lessons which he so generously gave.

If you have ever read the two-volume "Briefwechsel zwischen Wagner und Liszt" (Correspondence between Wagner and Liszt) you will see that Liszt was the most unselfish person in the world. Great as he was, he was willing to sacrifice himself for the sake of advancing the interests of the greater man — Wagner. In addition to the book I have just mentioned, if the Gentle Reader would like to look over a little book called "Der Kraft Mayr," by Ernst von Wolzogen, which has been fairly well translated under the title of "Florian Mayr," he might see how nearly like it was to my experience that Tuesday afternoon when the pupils came together. The pupils I mention in these reminiscences were not such a good lot as those who appear in the Florian book, but then, poetic license is always allowable.

To wind up my story about Joachim and his letter to Liszt: I left Berlin for Weimar that morning at a quarter before eight. At eight o'clock Joachim, having changed his mind about giving me the letter, went to my lodging to take it back, but it was too late. After my visit to Liszt at Weimar, I wrote to Joachim, putting my experience in as pleasant a light as possible. In any case, the following year, which I passed in Berlin, Joachim frequently asked me to come to his private rehearsals, sometimes telegraphing me at a moment's notice, so that I knew all was forgiven and forgotten. Joachim was the greatest violinist of his time. His playing of Beethoven's Concerto was generally accepted as a high-water mark of perfection. As an orchestral conductor he was never

35

a great success. He was probably too subjective. But as a leader of his Quartet,
when he *could* be subjective, he was un-
surpassed. The Helmesberger Quartet in
Vienna was more or less contemporaneous
with the Joachim Quartet and of the same
high order of interpretation. Both of these
quartets might be likened to our own
wonderful Flonzaleys.

Joachim was of large frame, had a big
head and lots of hair and a heavy beard.
He invariably wore a black frock coat and
a broad-brimmed black slouch hat. His
face was serious but benign. He never
seemed to be in a hurry, always having
time to be kind. He and Frau Joachim
lived for many years happily and artisti-
cally together. Afterwards, however, dif-
ferences arose which finally separated
them. Frau Joachim was a noted song
singer. She came to America in the late
eighties and gave a recital in Boston. She
asked me to accompany her, which I did
with pleasure and interest. We never referred to the late unpleasantness between

her and her husband. She was unlike
Leschetizky, who frequently spoke to me
of himself and Essipoff long after their
divorce and long after Leschetizky had
married again — several times.

LEAVING Weimar, my unprofessional companion and I went to Switzerland, joining
the friends with whom we had crossed the
ocean in the *Scythia* the year before. In
Geneva we found Phillips Brooks. Mr
Brooks knew the family with which we
were traveling. We therefore saw more or
less of him. We were looking forward to
hearing him preach Sunday morning but,
as the *Genevan Journal* said the next day:
"Owing to the breadth of Mr Brooks's
shoulders, the congregation lost the pleasure of hearing the breadth of his opinions."
As a matter of fact, the resident clergy-
man had no surplice large enough to cover
Mr Brooks's ample form.

Chamounix and Mont Blanc were our
next objective points. At Chamounix we
stayed two or three days. We didn't climb

Mont Blanc, but we saw it in all its glory, contenting ourselves by going over to Flégère and back to Montanvert, where we crossed the Mer de Glace. Our mule-back climb was another new experience. If you have ever taken a mule-back ride over a mountain pass, you will remember how a mule prefers to walk along the out-ermost edge of the precipice. I don't know why, but he does. From Chamounix, over the Tête Noir and the Simplon Pass, we went down to the Italian Lakes. That wonderland! There my unprofessional friend fell ill and we hurried on to Milan where we discovered that he had diphtheria. As the doctor refused to let me see him, I had to put in the time as well as I could. I think I saw every church and every picture in Milan. At the end of my friend's convalescence I ran up to Monte Generoso, north of Lake Como, to spend several days with Owen Wister. Monte Generoso was a lovely place, overlooking Lake Lugano. At the hotel we met some delightful English people with whom we made friends and with whom I dined, later, in London. Returning to Milan, I picked up my invalid and took him to Paris where we remained for a week or two. Then I went back to Berlin alone.

ARRIVING in Berlin, I found that Frau von Schack had made very different plans for the winter. An aunt had taken charge of the pension with Frau von Schack's daughters because Baron von Bleichröder had made Frau von Schack a handsome financial offer to become the head of his house and to take his daughter to Court. Von Bleichröder was a widower-millionaire, one of Bismarck's chief financial advisers. His palace was in the Behrenstrasse, and there Frau von Schack was given a suite of rooms with a carriage and a coachman, so that she might go and come as she pleased.

Fräulein von Bleichröder was not particularly attractive, nevertheless her father did everything to bring her forward before the world. There were grand dinners with

39

ambassadors and diplomats from all nations. Frau von Schack, being in charge of all arrangements, invited me to the dinners and to the musical parties and dances. One, in particular, I remember, when Sarasate and other great musical lights played and sang.

Frau von Schack, clinging still to the remains of her former glory, kept in touch with the royal family. On the birthday of Kaiser Wilhelm, she took me to the Kaiser's palace and let me see the presents displayed in one of the family rooms. The only presents I remember were different bronzes. On one of them was a card from the Crown Prince and the Grand Duchess of Baden (the Crown Prince's sister) on which was written: "Für Papa, von Fritz und Louisa" (For Papa, from Fritz and Louisa). On the card from the present ex-Kaiser — he was then about twenty-four — was written: "Für Kaiser Wilhelm von Seiner Königlichen, Kaiserlichen Hoheit, Prinz Wilhelm von Preussen" (For Kaiser William, from His Royal, Imperial Highness, Prince William of Prussia). Crown Prince Frederick was adored by everybody. The present-day ex-Kaiser got his deserts owing to his acute egoism.

On the evening of the Kaiser's birthday there was a brilliant celebration in the "Weisser Saal" (white ballroom) of the old palace, where the world assembled to honor the old Kaiser. An act was given from an opera, and a short play, and then by special permission. I took my place in a dance. Frau von Schack "tucked me in" the gallery where I could look over the whole scene. The costumes were brilliant. Those of the Hungarians seemed to me to be the most splendid. The old Kaiser was there, of course, and the Crown Prince and Princess, Bismarck and Moltke, too, and many other great people.

After two years of Frau von Schack's chaperonage in Baron von Bleichröder's palace, Fräulein von Bleichröder married an Austrian officer. Her father presented her with an estate in Silesia. The officer took his mistress along on his wedding

41

journey and placed her in a little house near the gate of the estate. Shortly after their marriage, the two were divorced. Frau von Schack returned to her simple life and her two daughters. In 1888 I stayed with them for several days as a guest, taking them to the opera and passing the time together pleasantly. Our correspondence continued for a while, irregularly, as correspondence of that sort languishes. In this case it ceased. Later on, my unprofessional friend returned to Berlin to see them on his travels. Frau von Schack had died, and her two daughters lived together very quietly in a remote quarter of Berlin. Since then I have heard nothing of them. My intimacy with the family of von Schack made a marked impression on my life.

During the last two or three months of my Berlin years I got to know a number of the members of the Mendelssohn family who had charming places at Charlottenburg, where we used to play tennis. One branch of the family had a splendid place

on the Rhine, nearly opposite Coblenz.
There I stayed a number of times subsequently. The Rhine flowed by and vine-
yards covered the hills. Felix Mendelssohn
spent much time there, writing his oratorio *St Paul* in the old garden house
where my host, in later years, made a
pastel portrait of me which he presented
to me and which I still have. There will
be further references to the Mendelssohn
family in these reminiscences.

As all things come to an end sooner or
later, my two years of Berlin life came to
an end too. In 1884 I returned to Boston
to take up my musical career, establishing
a permanent residence there. Having already known a good many Bostonians, I
soon found myself "in the swim." On
April 25, 1885, I made my first bow in
public before a Boston audience, bringing
out a lot of songs as a result of my study
in Berlin. Charles R. Adams was the
singer. He had been one of the leading
tenors in the Vienna Opera House. Hav-

43

ing begun, I continued to give a recital
nearly every year for more than twenty
years, for the sake of introducing my new
songs. I hated playing in public. I never
got over a temperamental nervousness.
Nevertheless, I played from time to time
in chamber concerts. Mrs Gardner invited
me and Charles M. Loeffler to play the
whole range of piano and violin sonatas in
her music room before about twenty-five
people each time. Bach, Mozart, Beethoven, Schumann, and Brahms — the series
lasted through four years. I like to recall
the names of the singers who used to sing
my songs: Lena Little, Julie Wyman,
Marie Brema, Eliot Hubbard, Max Heinrich, John S. Codman, Heinrich Meyn,
and others.

My next trip to Europe was in 1886,
when, after a while in London, I joined
my Mendelssohn friend, going to Bayreuth for *Parsifal* and *Tristan*. The performances that summer were splendid.
It was the year that Liszt died there. I was

unable to remain for the funeral owing to plans made for me by other people in Heidelberg for the celebration of the Five Hundredth Anniversary of the University; but Mrs Gardner, offering her homage, placed a laurel wreath on Liszt's grave, which made a great impression on the other mourners.

My Mendelssohn friend, being a student at Heidelberg, became my host for the fortnight of festivities there. Months before, two thousand costumes had been designed and made, representing different periods in the five centuries of the University. There was a great chronological pageant to open the ceremonies. After this opening, joy was unconfined. There were dinners and dinners and more dinners, with speeches and speeches and more speeches, and champagne and champagne and more champagne. Old, middle-aged, and young students came from everywhere to celebrate. The whole town was filled with students wearing the multi-colored caps of their different corps, some of them leading bulldogs on leash, and most of them proudly displaying their scars. My friend made me a temporary member of the corps to which he belonged, so I was taken into the student life which, apart from the dinners, consisted in drinking beer and singing songs. After the various dinners, in spite of having had more food and drink than was good for them, everybody repaired to the corps where most of the rest of the night was spent in the above-mentioned genial way. Nobody appeared until midday, when "Frühschoppen" (white wine and seltzer) were drunk and when the students compared headaches. There were some picturesque moments during the fortnight, as for instance, when the castle was illuminated, when rockets and Roman candles were shot out of the towers, and when the bridge over the Neckar down below looked like a blazing Niagara Falls. The same illumination took place on the last evening of the celebration when two thousand students in costume made merry all night. The inner courts were brilliantly lighted, tableaux were arranged, bands played, and of course there was no end of food and drink. On the "Great Tun" students danced, some of them challenging each other, planning for duels next day. As good luck would have it, a member of the corps of which I was a guest had been summoned to a funeral, so he offered me his costume, a suit of mail which I wore with great success.

After those two weeks of hilarity, it was no wonder I was glad to go with Mendelssohn to his quieter place on the Rhine, where I stayed for a week or more. Some of the Heidelberg students whom I had got to know came for a day or two, and we made merry all over again. While I was there, we spent a day going up the Mosel. The Mosel joins the Rhine near Coblenz. About twenty miles above the junction of the two rivers is Schloss Eltz, a wonderful old place belonging to the Counts Eltz, who have lived there ever since the tenth century. As we were only

47

tourists, we couldn't pay our respects to the family, but we saw the old Count sitting under his vine and fig tree.

In 1888, with Eliot Hubbard I sailed directly to France, planning first for a little trip through Normandy. The churches and the architecture of other old buildings and the Bayeux tapestry were interesting. Going west, we went to Mont St Michel, climbing to the top of it. On the shoulders of the "Marquis de Tamberlaine," a picturesque imaginary nobleman, we were carried safely, avoiding quicksands. At déjeuner, we had the best omelette ever made and chicken broiled by Madame Poulard, who was beautiful and adored by everyone who came to eat her omelettes and her broiled chicken. The walls of her inn were hung with pictures, painted by various artists and presented by them to Madame Poulard. We saw the tide coming in — a great sight! Standing on the ramparts, watching the tide, a native woman near us said, "Ah, Monsieur, vous pouvez

48

courir aussi vite que vous voulez, la Marée
vous attrapera toujours."

We stayed at Mont St Michel for a day
and a night and then, after a visit to Le
Mans and Chartres, we went to Paris.
After a few days in Paris, we went on to
Bayreuth by way of Strassburg. At Bayreuth *Die Meistersinger* was given and, of
course, *Parsifal*. On July 23 of that year,
Materna said, "That performance was so
wonderful it was as if it had been shot out
of a gun." That performance was considered the best of the summer. Materna was
the greatest of all Brünnhildes. When he
was looking for the person to sing and act
the part, Wagner, embracing her, said,
"Now I have at last found my Brünn-
hilde." Materna, too, was the greatest of
all Kundrys. During each week of performances, there was an evening party at
"Wahnfried," Wagner's house. When Mr
and Mrs Gardner were in Bayreuth, Gericke led them and several others to the
party. Materna sang a scene from *Gotter-
dämmerung*, and I shall never forget the

49

singing by Scheidemantel of Schubert's
"Sei mir gegrüsst." All the singers of the
opera were there, and lots of other people.
Frau Cosima received us graciously, particularly Mrs Gardner.

During the latter part of that summer
(1888), joining Gericke (everybody who
knows about the Boston Symphony Orchestra knows of Gericke's great work), I
went to Vienna, passing several days there,
part of the time staying with Materna at
her charming villa outside of the city. Materna was fond of ninepins, which we
played every day. It was amusing to see
her play ninepins *before* tea, while *after* tea,
having put her costume for the rôle of that
evening into the carriage, we all drove to
the opera house, Materna singing on the
stage while we sat in the audience. Materna was a genial hostess, rather inclined
to embonpoint, like most Wagner heroines.
I daresay it was not only a love of sport,
but a certain vanity about her weight,
that made her so fond of ninepins. At any
rate, she was a delightful person and cer-

tainly one of the greatest singing artists of all time.

Leaving Vienna, I stopped in Dresden with George Monks, then went on to Berlin, passing a week there reviving impressions made during the years 1882–1884 and renewing old friendship with the von Schack family. From Berlin I returned to Boston.

In 1890, after a month in Venice with Mr and Mrs Gardner at Palazzo Barbaro, I went to the Engadine, stopping at Promontogno for a day or two with my Mendelssohn friend. After that short stop, I continued up the valley to St Moritz, where I lived for a time at the Kulm Hotel. After dinner one day, a heavy snowstorm being then in progress (in August), I espied a familiar figure muffled to the chin, covered with snow. I inquired of the man at the door whether that was not Herr Joachim. The man said it was. Joachim soon set himself to rights and we sat together while he dined. He then proposed we should both go back to Promon-

togno and celebrate "Charlie's" birthday,
Charlie being my Mendelssohn friend and
an old friend of Joachim's. Joachim was on
his way to Italy, to stay with Piatti, the
celebrated 'cellist. Joachim said he would
wait over a day or two at Promontogno if
I would do the same. Back we went and
had a great time celebrating the birthday.
The next day, Joachim, offering to play
anything we wanted to hear, took us to
his room and played the "Chaconne" and
a number of other pieces by Bach and the
old Italians. After the music, we climbed
up to Soglio where we lunched on the
mountainside and had ourselves photographed. The third day Joachim went
south, and I returned to St Moritz.

As there are so many references in my
reminiscences to Palazzo Barbaro, may I
say that it is a splendid palace on the
Grand Canal, originally belonging to one
of the Doges. In later years it was the
property of Mr and Mrs Daniel Curtis.
For a number of seasons Mr and Mrs
Gardner hired it for the summer during

the absence of the owners. It now belongs to, and is occupied by Mrs Ralph Curtis, the daughter-in-law of the late Mr and Mrs Curtis. It was my good fortune to be invited by Mr and Mrs Gardner to stay a number of times there. Both he and she loved the place, and no wonder!

My reminiscences of 1891 begin, like charity, at home. A musical meteor appeared in Boston in the person of Paderewski. We had never heard anybody like him before; in fact, we never have since. Paderewski gave a series of recitals. I shall never forget my first impressions of his playing. When he came to Boston, he always stayed at the Hotel Brunswick. After each recital he asked a lot of us, ten or a dozen, to dine with him. Prohibition hadn't been invented, so champagne flowed freely. Up to the morning hours everybody played poker. Bridge was not known. A darkey attached to the hotel was in constant attendance. Paderewski always called him General Washington.

Mrs Gardner, wishing to be individual as she wished always to be individual in everything she did, engaged Paderewski to play a recital for herself alone at her house, 152 Beacon-street. Before the recital, Mrs Gardner, out of the kindness of her heart, smuggled me into an adjoining room where I sat and listened behind the tapestries. After the music was over, I was invited to join the supper party which was composed of Mr and Mrs Gardner, Paderewski, and myself.

The Gardners' house was filled with beautiful things. The music room was charming, with acoustics unusually good. Number 152 Beacon-street no longer exists. Mrs Gardner didn't want to have anybody *else* live in it, so it was demolished. After "the Flight of the Goddess," she alighted in the Fens, where she built her palace called Fenway Court. (If any curious person would take the trouble, he could see that the numbers in Beacon-street are now 150 and 154, *not* 152.)

A few days after her "lone recital," Mrs

54

MRS GARDNER'S MUSIC ROOM
AT 152 BEACON-STREET

Gardner engaged Paderewski to give another, this time for Boston's musicians and students in a hall more or less like an amphitheatre. Paderewski sat and played in the pit while the audience filled the seats in rising tiers. It was a great opportunity for the students, and it was certainly a splendid offering on the part of Mrs Gardner.

In addition to the Paderewski feasts at the Brunswick, Mr and Mrs Montgomery Sears gave wonderful musical parties. One in particular was in honor of Mr Sears's birthday. Paderewski was in Portland but expected to arrive in Boston in plenty of time for the party. An unexpected blizzard held up all trains. Paderewski, being determined not to disappoint Mr Sears, chartered a single locomotive without cars, in which he was carried from Portland to Boston, and in which he arrived just in time to play for the guests already assembled.

That season of 1891 was a banner year in Boston, but there were a great many more banner years when Mr and Mrs Sears entertained so lavishly. They had a big house and a big music room. Melba, Plançon, and any number of other great artists sang and played there. Mr and Mrs Sears loved entertaining as much as their guests loved to be entertained, while the artists loved to sing and play because the host and hostess and guests loved to hear them.

EIGHTEEN NINETY-Two brought Dvorák to America. Mrs Thurber, the wife of a millionaire merchant in New York, engaged the composer to be head of a school called "The National Conservatory of Music." Mr Thurber gave his wife a free hand to do as she pleased. She founded not only a school but also a "National Opera." For a time — a short time — they both flourished. Dvorák was a peasant and had no particular interest in conservatory management nor in teaching students. After three years in New York he returned to his native Bohemia. While he was in this country, he came to Boston to conduct his "Requiem," sung by the Cecilia Society. Having been engaged by the Cecilia, he was invited also by the Harvard Musical Association in Chestnut-street to a reception given by members and friends of the Association. Miss Lena Little and I were asked to sing and play a group of Dvorák's songs as a compliment to the composer. Miss Little had chosen several of Dvorák's important songs, one in particular. When we asked him if he would like to play the accompaniment himself, he looked at it and said, "I never saw it before. I never wrote it." The result was that I had to play the accompaniment to Miss Little's singing. Undoubtedly composers often forget their minor works. The whole world knows the Symphony "From the New World," and many music lovers know Dvorák's "D minor Symphony" and his chamber music. Some of his songs have great beauty — "Als die alte Mutter," for instance. Miss Little and I used to give a great many recitals, when she always sang songs of mine. She was a real artist and interpreter. I owe a great debt to her interest in the furtherance of my songs.

In the summer of 1892, when Paderewski was living in Paris, Mr and Mrs Sears happened to be there, too, wining and dining with him. I was invited to join them. There was one red-letter day when Paderewski asked us to drive out to St Cloud to see and meet Gounod. We left Paris about eleven o'clock, stopping at Munkácsy's studio, where the painter showed us his pictures and decorations. One great panel in particular was destined for the House of Parliament at Budapest. From the studio we went on to St Cloud, lunching there. The weather could hardly have been better. The view from Gounod's villa, looking over Paris, was wonderful. Monsieur and Madame Gounod were both charming. Paderewski, on the way from Paris, said that Gounod sang his own songs as no one else could. Gounod wanted to hear some Mozart. Paderewski played some Mozart, and then

GOUNOD

Gounod, in his half-voice, sang several of his songs. I begged Gounod to give me a photograph in memory of our visit. He gave me a personally inscribed amateur print: Gounod sitting on his piazza. When Madame Gounod saw the signed photograph she said, "Oh! That's the only one I've got and I can't get any more." I was sorry for Madame Gounod, but glad for the good luck which came my way.

In '94 William R. Mercer, my quasi-professional artist friend, asked me to join him in a trip down the Danube in a roughly-put-together houseboat which he had constructed with the assistance of a boatman. The boat was about sixty feet long and on it were four partitions. One served as a kitchen; in the others we slept. The only means of locomotion we had was the current of the river, which was often swift. At either end of the boat were long sweeps by which the craft was steered. Now and then we slept at little inns ashore. One was called "The Beautiful Blue Danube." The landlady's daughter played the zither and sang Tyrolean songs.

We drifted five hundred miles down the Danube, and the trip lasted about four weeks. Nearly two hundred and fifty miles above Vienna the Isar ("rolling rapidly") joins the larger river. From that point on, the water of the Isar combined with the waters of the Danube is like sizzling Apollinaris, owing possibly to the glacial water coming down from the Bavarian mountains. At Grein, considerably lower down, is the famous "Strudel" (whirlpool) where a number of wrecks had occurred. We were not allowed to pass through the whirlpool without taking government boatmen on board. Luckily nothing untoward happened to us.

The Danube is more picturesque than the Rhine; the hills are higher and on many of them castles perch. There are also many churches and shrines. We saw a long procession coming down a hill to the riverside from one of the shrines. The pilgrims were singing and carrying ban-

ners in honor of a saint's day. The leader
of the procession was so drunk he hardly
held up the crucifix he carried. Most Aus-
trians are genial, and many are devout.

At another time, when we had some
trouble about the boat which had been
carried too far by the current, we had to
drag it back. An obliging boatman in-
sisted upon helping us; he too, however,
was so drunk he fell down every few steps.
He then apologetically said: "Ich gehe
nicht sehr gut mit diesen Stiefeln" (I
don't walk very well in these boots). We
saw only an occasional boat between Linz
and Vienna. This stretch of the river was
very different from the Rhine, which is
crowded with all sorts of traffic.

Leaving the Danube, I joined Mr and
Mrs Gardner at Ischl, meaning to stop
there two or three days before going to
Venice. Gericke, who was living at Steinkogl, took us to see Brahms. Gericke, leading the way, cried out through the open
door, "Amerika kommt" (America is coming). Brahms understood, "Mrs Gardner

61

kommt," so by the misunderstanding the ice was broken. We stayed only for a few minutes. Brahms spoke no English and Mrs Gardner no German, so Gericke became interpreter. I don't remember what anybody said, but we *saw* Brahms in his little roadside house, the simplest little house you ever saw, and that was the main thing.

A year later I saw a great deal of Brahms. One day he gave me a big black cigar, the first among many others. Instead of smoking it, I kept it as a souvenir. After having brought it back to Boston, I placed it under a glass case with an old clock. There it remained for many years. Alas! in 1911 I was obliged to move my lodgings, owing to the extension of the State House, and in the moving, the cigar was lost. Now there is only a recollection of it. Had I smoked it, I might at least have kept the ashes.

In the early years of my London experiences, a well-known lady of Boston, Mrs Charles Dorr, gave me a letter of introduction to the Marchioness of Waterford. Mrs

Dorr and Lady Waterford had at one time
happened to be on the Nile, tied up in
dahabeahs, side by side. In the course of
conversation Lady Waterford asked Mrs
Dorr if she knew Mr Clayton Johns. Mrs
Dorr allowed she did. As Lady Waterford
was musically inclined, and wrote songs
herself, she knew a song of mine called
"The Scythe Song" which she liked. The
upshot of it all was that I saw something
of Lady Waterford in London. She asked
me to do pleasant things, making and
talking about music. When I first met
her, she was a perfect type of "grande
dame," tall, beautiful, and splendid-look-
ing. A year or two later she began to be ill.
Nevertheless, she was able to go yachting
and to go to Ireland, where Lord Waterford had a noted place, "Curraghmore,"
to which she asked me to come for a visit
on my way to America. Just before sailing,
I saw in the newspapers a report that Lord
Waterford had shot himself, so I ante-
dated my letter, pretending not to have
heard anything about the tragedy, regret-

ting that I couldn't accept the kind invitation to Curraghmore. Shortly afterwards, Lady Waterford died herself, but I still have "Four Songs" of hers and a number of letters and a beautiful photograph. Perhaps I may be forgiven a personal note here, and add that Mrs Gardner also always liked my "Scythe Song" better than any other.

By way of an interlude, let me say a word about Mrs Gardner, who so often is mentioned in these reminiscences. She belonged to the world of rare achievement. Her chief interests were associated with musicians, painters, and literary men. Her crowning glory was the creation of her Venetian palace, originally called "Fenway Court," which she presented to the city and public as an enduring monument of her love of art. The inception of her idea, building a palace of her own, came long before the thought of taking the Palazzo Barbaro in Venice for the summer, which she did over and over again, beginning in 1890. The world now knows what the "Isabella Stewart Gardner Museum" means and always will mean for Boston: a wonderful collection of paintings and beautiful things of all sorts. Mrs Gardner once said, "Instead of building hospitals, I am going to try to make the world more beautiful." She did. When Fenway Court was finished, Mr Gericke, conducting the Boston Symphony Orchestra, dedicated it by giving a concert before several hundred friends of Mrs Gardner's in the new music room. Afterwards Gericke said, "Mrs Gardner is a genius lady." She certainly was. She had no beauty of face, but a wonderful and illuminating personality which drew about her all sorts and conditions of men and women. She was interested in everything that was interesting and in everybody who interested her. She had the power of getting the best out of each thing and person. She had a marvelous determination about anything she *wanted* to do. When she broke her ankle, years ago, she

was carried up in a hammock by her servants to the balcony in the old Music Hall,
where she appeared at every concert. She
knew no obstacle; in fact, obstacles were
to her an inspiration. Her own charm,
with her beautiful surroundings, formed
an unforgettable atmosphere of music,
flowers, and art.

THERE was another great soul in Boston:
Henry Lee Higginson, founder of the Symphony Orchestra. Like Mrs Gardner,
dreaming of building and filling with
beautiful pictures a palace of her own,
Mr Higginson dreamed of founding an
orchestra to provide Boston with beautiful music. Both dreams came true. For
nearly forty years Mr Higginson sup-
ported the orchestra, raising it to a
world's standard. Orchestral conductors
might come and orchestral conductors
might go, but Mr Higginson stuck to his
original purpose, until a short time before
his death, when his mantle was passed on
to other shoulders.

66

I like to remember Nikisch, who succeeded Gericke with the Boston Symphony Orchestra in 1889. Mr Higginson asked me to stay for a week at his place by the sea with Nikisch, just arrived. Mrs Higginson was away and Mr Higginson busy in town, so I was left to look after Nikisch. We talked and walked and drove. Nikisch spoke hardly any English, but his keen sense of sound enabled him soon to speak correctly and, above all, to *listen* attentively. I remember he once said, "Englisch ist eine verfluchte Sprache" (cursed language). "The judge judges and the judges judge." On the other hand, he found "charming" such a charming word. He couldn't comprehend "Amerikanische Freiheit" (American freedom), as for instance, when everybody is allowed to do as he pleases, even to walking on the railroad track at his own risk. Near Mr Higginson's place was a railroad on which we walked by the side of the track. When we heard a whistle in the distance, Nikisch was "scared blue," ran up the hill, and climbed over a fence. The old German "protection" was sometimes a good thing. I often wish we might have a little more of it. In addition to his orchestral powers, Nikisch played the piano beautifully, so we had music in the evening. We all know how well he led the Boston Orchestra for a number of years. In 1893 he returned to Europe. Seventeen years later he again came to America, conducting the London Symphony Orchestra, touring all over the United States.

In a lighter vein, Mr Higginson was for twenty years president of the "Tavern Club," a little club formed for the enjoyment of music and good-fellowship. Gericke, coming to Boston at the time the club started, took an active part in the entertainments. Paderewski spent much time there, playing billiards and the piano. The de Reszkes sang, Salvini and Coquelin dined, wined, and recited, and a host of other celebrities shared the club's hospitality. Even Lilli Lehmann ("no ladies admitted"), having said, "I want to go

to the Tavern Club," went, sang, and (if
I remember rightly) danced, taking with
her a few choice spirits. The Tavern Club
and the Boston Symphony Orchestra were
young in those days. May the club and
the harvest of Mr Higginson's well-sown
seed last for many a day.

AMONG other interesting houses in the Boston of those days let me not forget that of
Mr and Mrs Apthorp. For many years
their Sunday evenings were unique. Many
times during the winter they gave little
dinners of six or eight people, usually having some "high-light" guest like Paderewski, Melba, Sarah Bernhardt, Coquelin,
or Salvini. After dinner, special friends
were invited to meet the honored guest.
Mrs Gardner and Gericke were always
there. Besides, there were members of the
younger set — youth and beauty for dec-
oration. Mr and Mrs Apthorp were rare
entertainers, given to hospitality in its
best sense. Later in the evening, beer and
cigars lent a Bohemian air to the occa-

sions. Mrs Apthorp appeared, carrying a large pitcher of beer in one hand, beer mugs hanging from each finger of her other hand. As Blue Laws still obtained, dancing was not allowed until after midnight, but *then* it was "On with the dance."

Mr and Mrs Dixey didn't entertain in a large way, but they gave charming dinners of ten or a dozen, frequently. Mr Dixey was a lover of music and Mrs Dixey a lover of all things beautiful; they entertained artists, musicians, and the beau monde. Let me recall one evening when Lilli Lehmann was the chief guest. Her sister Marie and Van Dyck were there, also the Gerickes and others. After dinner, Gericke, seating himself at the piano, played bits of Wagner. Lehmann thereupon began to sing *Tristan und Isolde*. Becoming more and more inspired, she sang the whole of Isolde's death scene. As the company was getting a little too serious, Lilli asked for a broom. Astride the broomstick she sang and acted the witch's dance from *Hänsel und Gretel*.

Hilarity then knew no bounds. Staid matrons and maids joined in the dance. I remember one imitated a can-can.

HAVING made many references to Wilhelm Gericke, may I add a few personal words about him? Gericke was the father of the Boston Symphony Orchestra. He held the post of conductor longer than any successor. His name is still one to conjure with. When he came to Boston from Vienna, where he had been one of the conductors of the opera, he was just forty. Mr Higginson spoke of him as an "Ehrenmann" (man of honor) which he was and always remained. What Gericke did we all know. The proof of the pudding is the eating of it. His pudding was good and we all enjoyed it for many years. When he came, in 1884, I had just returned from Berlin after my two years of study there. We both immediately became members of the Tavern Club where we lived in daily intercourse. Gericke spoke but little English. I, after my training under Frau Dr

Hempel, talked German only with him, which was a strong bond.

Every Saturday night all music lovers, members of the Tavern Club, used to come back after the Symphony Concert for supper at the Tavern. Mr Higginson was always there. He and Gericke had much to talk over. Gericke was a bachelor, and we were all young, so we didn't care whether we went to bed early or not. We had many genial evenings. The special evenings were celebrated at Christmas and at "Narrenabend" (All Fools' Night). In those days the world was not ashamed to mention a German word. Gericke was the moving musical spirit on all these occasions. No matter how tired he might be after rehearsals, he was always ready to take part in any spree. On one of the Narrenabends there was a "Dime Museum" in which Gericke, décolleté, with his black beard, was exhibited as "Madame Pastrana, the Bearded Lady, commonly called Herr (Hair) Gericke." That performance took place in Vinton's studio, before we had a whole house of our own. I remember another evening in Vinton's studio when Henry Irving was the guest of honor, when he sat up until five, as the rest of us often did; but I mustn't digress. I am thinking only of Gericke.

Those were young and careless days, when life was constantly on the move. The winters were full of interest. The summers were usually spent in Europe. After the musical season was ended, Mrs Gardner, every year, asked Gericke and me to pass a week with her and Mr Gardner at "Green Hill" in Brookline. After breakfast Gericke and I took a long walk. The rest of the day was spent in various pleasures provided by our host and hostess. Green Hill was one of the loveliest places near Boston, with a charming house and music room, splendid trees, beautiful flowers, Japanese irises, and a Chinese water garden. From the hill there was a hazy atmospheric view over Boston. People came and went. Mrs Gardner was never at a loss to entertain herself and her

73

friends. Those were halcyon days when Russell Sullivan and I called Mrs Gardner "The Queen" while Gericke was her "Kapellmeister."

DURING the summer of 1895 I passed six weeks in London, seeing many people and hearing much music. A number of my songs were sung by Melba, Emma Eames, Marie Brema, David Bispham, Theodore Byard and others, in public and private. I always played the accompaniments. Sometimes I took part in two or three different concerts in a single afternoon, driving from one just in time to appear on the stage for the next.

Emma Eames was a woman of unusual beauty, with a beautiful voice. She became a star shining over two continents, where she triumphed in Paris, London, New York, Boston, and all the chief cities of the United States. Many people remember how beautiful she was as Juliet and as the Countess in *The Marriage of Figaro*. I first met and heard her at a musical

74

MRS GARDNER

party given by Mr and Mrs Winthrop
Sargent of Boston. They were giving a
housewarming. All society was there. One
room, leading out of the music room, was
unfinished but had been converted into a
palm garden temporarily. Arthur Rotch,
the brother of Mrs Sargent and the archi-
tect of the house, led Miss Eames all
about on his arm. Passing in the throng,
I overheard her say, "I never saw so many
spoon corners in all my life!" Miss Eames
was just nineteen and radiantly beautiful.
After her successes on the stage she re-
tired to private life, living for some years
in her native town of Bath, Maine. She
has now established herself in Paris,
permanently.

But to return to London: While singing
at Covent Garden in the season of '95,
Melba took a place on the river about
twenty miles from London. Here she
asked me and a number of other friends
to pass Sunday now and then. One Sunday, particularly, Melba hired a steam
launch in which we spent most of the day,

lunching on board under the trees. That day everybody had lunched excepting Maurel, who arrived an hour or two late. Maurel, being the greatest singing actor of our time, was "spoiled" and usually got what he wanted. So everything had to be rearranged for another meal while the entire company had to watch him eat and drink. A few days later Melba was giving a luncheon of fourteen at the Savoy Hotel, the guests being Marchesi, the Tostis, Calvé, and others. This time, Maurel didn't come at all, to the consternation of the company, for no one was willing to sit down with thirteen; so a small table was placed near by where two guests at a time took turns breaking the spell. Maurel had a personal charm added to his great art, and his hostess readily forgave him.

Another Sunday on the river Paderewski and the Nikisches were in the same steam launch. Melba was again hostess. Paderewski wore his usual frock coat, silk hat, and voluminous white necktie. It was small wonder that he attracted general attention to the holiday makers. At a landing near one of the inns on the river a collision occurred between the boats. A chair tumbled overboard, and at the same time Mrs Nikisch tumbled *in*. She suffered nothing more serious than a ducking, however, as she was promptly rescued. After that delightful day, Paderewski returned directly to London, while I stayed to dine, taking a later train in time to go to Madame ——'s, where Paderewski played.

Melba was the greatest lyric soprano of her time; she was also a most genial and hospitable hostess. She loved having people about her and doing kind things for others. I am glad to have known her for a number of years both in Boston and in London, where I found her always a good friend.

John Sargent, whom I used to see often in London, once asked me to spend a day with the Royal Academy of Painters on their annual outing. We went to Lord Salisbury's place at Hatfield, not far from London. After having lunched we stretched

77

ourselves on the grass under the trees,
smoking and chatting. Du Maurier was
there. "Trilby" was a new sensation. Sargent told me of a conversation he had
with du Maurier about Whistler. Du
Maurier had supposed that he and Whistler were friends. Whistler said that he
hadn't been a friend of du Maurier's for
the last thirty years. Du Maurier was
much grieved by Whistler's treatment.
Those who read "Trilby" at that time
will know of the difference that existed
between the two men. Later in the day
there was an elaborate dinner at the inn,
where Alma Tadema presided, making
amusing speeches. Sargent was toasted
as the representative American painter.

Long before, and long after, that pleasant
day I saw much of Sargent, both at home
and abroad. At the time of the first instal-
ment of his decorations for the Boston
Public Library, the library was opened by
a formal supper of one hundred and fifty
persons of both sexes. The architects of

78

the library, Messrs McKim, Mead, and White, were there. Sargent was toasted. He hated being toasted because it was an agony for him to have to respond. On that occasion, slowly rising and grasping the table, he began: "I want — I want — Mr — Mr Mead — Mr — Mr — White —Mr Mead." With that he sat down. As we walked home together, Sargent said, "Wasn't it awful!"

Sargent's "word portraits" were as remarkable as his painted portraits. I remember the descriptions he gave of Lady Faudel-Phillips, the Lady Mayoress, in her flesh and diamonds, and of different members of the Wertheimer family, of whom he painted eleven.

From time to time in London I dined with Sargent and his mother and sister, who lived in Chelsea near Sargent's house at 31 Tite-street. After dinner we all went to the theatre or opera. After the performance, the ladies went home while Sargent and I went off for a bit of supper. That was the time when he was at

79

his best, talking about music, books, people, and his work. On one of these occasions I caught him looking attentively at a man sitting at a near-by table. I asked if the man would make a good prophet. Sargent thought he might. At that time Sargent had been over in Amsterdam looking for Jewish types, so his mind was full of them. In those days he led a quiet life, seeing a few intimate friends, most of them musically inclined — Henschel, Shakespeare, Korbay and others. Sargent had a keen interest in music. He liked playing what is called "four hands." Also he liked to play chess. As time went on, he mingled more in the great world, but music continued to be his second love up to the last. Sargent had an unusual personality, and I am proud to have known him intimately for nearly forty years. May I close a pen-picture of him by recalling an incident which he told me in connection with the Boston Public Library and its committee? In the beginnings of the library, Whistler was asked

JOHN SINGER SARGENT
After the Crayon Portrait by Raymond Crosby

by the committee to decorate the north wall of Bates Hall. When the committee said, however, that they would be very glad indeed to have a *serious* work by Mr Whistler, Whistler retorted: "I thank you, gentlemen, but it would be impossible to change the traditions of a lifetime." If anybody should wonder why that north-wall panel remains undecorated, let him be referred to the above incident.

One evening Henschel invited me to dine at his house. Among the guests were Sir Hubert Parry, Villiers Stanford, Barnby, Shakespeare, Bispham, Alma Tadema, Arthur Foote, and others. Henschel was the first conductor of the Boston Symphony Orchestra, which he led for three years, from 1881 to 1884. He and Mrs Henschel used to give song recitals — beautiful programmes, beautifully sung. On his return to London he took a charming house and music room in St John's Wood. His little dinner parties and his Sunday afternoons, when great artists sang and played, were delightful. He must now be nearly eighty, but until recently he sang in public.

Thanks to Sargent's kindness, I was often at Alma Tadema's, dining there now and then, and going to Mrs Tadema's evening parties with music. The grand piano in the music room was a souvenir piano, the inside of the lid being scratched over with innumerable names of musicians — Paderewski's and all the others. Tadema's house was original, architecturally and decoratively. The decorations were all done by Tadema himself. At one of the evening parties, standing near Mrs Gardner, as she said farewell (she was leaving London the next day), I overheard her say: "Oh! Mr Tadema, I'm afraid this is good night and good-bye." "Good God!" said Tadema. Tadema was a genial host; he loved people and people loved to go to his house.

AFTER those busy days in London I went to Ischl, remaining there for six weeks, taking a lodging, hiring a piano, meaning

to do some work. The summer of 1895 was
a high-water mark for Ischl. Brahms was
there as usual; Leschetizky in his house;
Johann Strauss at his charming villa. Such
a galaxy of celebrities drew crowds of musicians. The Gerickes were near by at
Steinkogl. The Nikisches came for a few
days. The Kneisel Quartet took a house
for the summer. Mahler, Eduard Schuett,
and a number of others turned up. At the
little café on the esplanade by the river all
the musicians assembled at a long table,
Brahms sitting at one end. Brahms had an
enormous head, a large body, and very
short legs, looking very small as to height.
He always wore Jaeger clothing, outside
and in. His manner was variable, sometimes genial and at others quite the opposite. As an instance of his temper, when
we were all going to his new house to hear
his new clarinet sonatas, to be played by
him and Mühlfeld, Fräulein Eibenschütz
asked if she might be there, too. Brahms
gruffly said: "Ich spiele nicht vor Klavier-
spielern" (I don't play before pianists).

Fräulein Eibenschütz's feelings were hurt,
and she wept in a corner alone until
Schuett tried to console her. Brahms and
Eibenschütz made it up later, however,
when she played his G minor pianoforte
quartet at a party at Johann Strauss's to
celebrate Brahms's birthday. He and
Strauss were great friends. I was often at
the Strauss villa. Frau Strauss and her
daughter were socially inclined, so I
dropped in to tea now and then. Strauss
was there sometimes, smoking his long
hookah.

Leschetizky held a court all his own. He
and Brahms were on amiable terms but
not intimate. I never saw them together,
nor did I ever see Leschetizky with
Strauss. Leschetizky was not at the
Brahms-Strauss party. Nobody could
have been more delightful and interesting
than Leschetizky. I took long walks with
him, frequently dining with him at his
house. The day before I left Ischl he
played for me an hour or two, all sorts of
pieces. He said he hadn't played for any-

body for years. He always had something interesting or amusing to say when I met him.

We had a number of other musical afternoons, either at Brahms's house or at Kneisel's, when Brahms or Nikisch played the piano part of his quartets or quintet. Brahms's playing was rather stiff and old-fashioned. I remember his playing his D minor pianoforte concerto in Berlin in 1884, before conducting his "Third Symphony" on the same programme. Piano playing at that time was not what it now is, but there was a halo of glory over Brahms as pianist and composer. I can now only think of it as a great occasion. During those six weeks in Ischl I was in daily intercourse with all the musicians of whom I speak — not on hob-nobbing terms with Brahms, of course, but at the same table with him almost every day. Before I left Ischl, I went to see him at his house, to say good-bye and to ask him to sign a photograph of himself. As I held the picture out to him, Brahms said mod-

estly, "Darf ich meinen Namen darauf
schreiben?" (May I write my name on
it?) I have that photograph on my wall
hanging next to the one of Gounod.

In 1897, like "Three Men on a Bummel"
we went bicycling in England and France,
not hearing much music but seeing a great
deal of the so-called frozen kind in the
shape of cathedrals and châteaux. Once
more we spent a day or two at Mont St
Michel, where we once more ate an omelette made by Madame Poulard. After
penetrating a little into Brittany, we
turned back into Touraine, following the
Loire. From Chartres we continued on to
Paris. Leaving Paris, I again stayed with
Mr and Mrs Gardner in Venice. One evening during my visit Mrs Gardner hired a
barca (a barca is much larger than a gondola). A piano was put on board, and the
barca was propelled by gondoliers. The
company having been comfortably seated,
Theodore Byard (one of my "bummeling"
companions) and I gave a concert, going

BRAHMS

up and down the Grand Canal, gondolas following the barca. We might have collected quite a sum for charity, but we didn't.

In 1899, sailing from New York in May, I found on board Antonio de Navarro and his wife, Mary Anderson, the most beautiful woman on the stage. When we arrived in England, they asked me to stay with them at their place "Court Farm," Broadway, Worcestershire — a charming house and garden, in an old Elizabethan village. I remained there for ten days, doing all sorts of pleasant things. Watching cricket was the chief amusement, with matches between musicians, painters, and literary men. The musicians were Plunkett Greene and Kennerly Rumford. Several of the artists belonged to the staff of *Punch*. The literary men were Augustine Birrell, J. M. Barrie and others. Frank Millet and Navarro were the special hosts. After the cricket week was over, there was a grand dinner party of fifty in the old priory, re-

stored by Millet and belonging to him.
The hostesses, Mrs Millet and Mrs de
Navarro, were toasted. At one end of the
long table stood Mrs Millet taking the
arm of Birrell. Birrell responded for her.
In like manner Mrs de Navarro took the
arm of Barrie while Barrie responded for
her. I remember how brilliant the speeches
were. Of course, there was a dance in
Millet's studio lasting most of the night.

When the festivities had quieted down,
I stayed on at Court Farm for several
days. In the good old times of bicycling
Navarro and I went a-wheeling all over
the shire, going to Stratford-on-Avon,
Warwick Castle, and many other places.
During cricket week, Maude Valerie
White sprained her ankle, which caused
her to be laid up for some time. Miss
White was a delightful person and most
amusing, belonging to the late Victorian
period of music. Her songs had a great
vogue sung by Marie Brema, Plunkett
Greene, and everybody else. On account
of her lame ankle, she remained in bed.

Her house was next to Court Farm, and we used to go up to her room after dinner. Her spirits were not dampened by her accident. Being a great mimic, while lying in bed she imitated Queen Victoria. Putting a soap dish on her head for a crown, and hanging from the soap dish a towel for a widow's weed, she stuck her forefinger in her cheek and gazed at the picture of the Prince Consort, thus making a perfect likeness of the well-known photograph of the Queen.

Miss White was a wonderful talker, in a good sense. Once I said to Mrs de Navarro, "I am sure Miss White never married because she has never given any man the chance to propose." The next day, Mrs de Navarro and I were walking under Miss White's window. Miss White called down and said, "Tell Mr Johns that England expects every man to do his duty." The next day I returned to London, so I never had a chance to propose.

A few years later I was again staying at Court Farm with the de Navarros. The

Dowager Countess of Strathmore and her daughter, Lady Maud Bowes-Lyon, took a place next to Court Farm. Lady Maud, who was a good amateur violinist, and I made a good deal of music together — Brahms's sonatas and other things. Both of the ladies were charming. Mrs de Navarro had often told me of her visits to Glamis Castle, belonging to the Earl of Strathmore. Everybody has heard of Glamis Castle, with its "monster" (or, as it was called by the knowing ones, "the ghost"), shedding gloom over the place and over everybody in it, guests and everyone else. Mrs de Navarro said that the sinister influence was indefinable, only it was there. I was interested to see the Countess of Strathmore, in her simple surroundings at Broadway, where she seemed to be one of the most calm and serene persons imaginable in spite of the shadow cast by the "monster" during her married life. The Dowager Countess of Strathmore is the mother of the Earl of Strathmore, and the grandmother of the Duchess of

MARY ANDERSON DE NAVARRO

York. Recently I heard that the "monster" had died or been done away with in some way.

Mary Anderson was not only the most beautiful woman on the stage but was of the most beautiful spirit, kind and thoughtful to everybody, devoted to her husband, children, and friends. She forsook the stage without a pang because she chose the better part. Her marriage was ideal. During the World War she played a number of times, at the Stratford Theatre, in London, in Manchester, in fact all over England and Scotland, for the sake of the common cause, realizing the sum of £48,000 ($240,000).*

For a few weeks after my first visit to Court Farm I lingered in London and then went over to Paris where the Venezuelan

*In a letter, after having read my reminiscences in manuscript, Bishop Lawrence said: "I have read with much interest and pleasure your Reminiscences. What privilege of comradeship and friendship you have had with the great musicians and others! The one whom I should like to have met especially was Mary Anderson."

91

Tribunal was in session. Ex-President Harrison presented the case for the United States, and my brother-in-law, Severo Mallet-Prevost, assisted him. I had the opportunity of going to some of the hearings and more particularly going to the dinners and seeing more or less of the English representatives with their families — Lord and Lady Russell of Killowen with their daughters and Lord Justice and Lady Collins with *their* daughters. The case was decided by compromise, as many cases have been decided before and since. Having passed two or three weeks in Paris, I went bicycling again with L. F. over the northeastern part of France — France long before the devastation. We saw Amiens, Beauvais, Soissons, Laon, Rheims, and a lot of other places. Later I went to St Moritz, where I had been so often; a place which always seemed to me a happy hunting ground for doing pleasant things and seeing agreeable people.

During one of my visits at St Moritz there was a great dinner at the Palace

Hotel. The Palace is a little below the Kulm (where I always stayed), between the Kulm and the Lake. The Duchess of Aosta was the guest of honor. When the Duchess arrived, everybody stood up, of course, and remained standing until the Duchess took her seat. There were representatives of many countries. Reverence was duly paid to blood royal. St Moritz is a cosmopolitan place. I remember a picnic in the woods when charming people coming together made a company of eleven different nations.

THE same year of my visit to Broadway — 1899 — I paid a visit to Longford Castle, a great place near Salisbury with a celebrated collection of pictures. The collection is still wonderful but "The Admiral" by Velasquez, "The Ambassadors" by Holbein, and a portrait by Moroni were bought by the authorities of the National Gallery some years ago. My hostess was the Countess of Radnor, another remarkable woman, whom I have

93

had the honor of knowing for thirty years and who has meant much to me in my life.

Leaving London for Longford Castle, I found a number of persons in the train who were going to join the house party. After our hostess had received us and had given us tea, a servant, leading up to my room, handed me a printed plan of the castle which I kept during my visit in order not to lose my way. After dinner we had a delightful evening — cards and chat. The next morning, my hostess led me through the halls and rooms, showing me the pictures. Opening a large gilt cabinet with a gold key, she said, "These things are very precious because they all belonged to Queen Elizabeth." I wish I could remember all the beautiful things I saw there. Queen Elizabeth once stayed at Longford Castle. I don't know how long *she* stayed, but *I* stayed nearly three days.

Not like Mrs Gardner, who never did anything in the way of singing, playing, or painting herself — only inspired other people to do things — Lady Radnor sang, played, painted, and conducted a chorus and an orchestra of amateurs which she formed herself in behalf of her daughter, the Countess of Lathom, giving, under the patronage of the Queen, an annual concert in London for the benefit of hospitals. In Venice, taking a palace on the Grand Canal, she trained a chorus, doing much good trying to improve the musical conditions of the "singing boats" which sometimes make confusion worse confounded. In 1900 she planned a concert of my songs to be sung by different singers in London, at Stafford House, the Duke of Sutherland's. The concert, unhappily, never came off, owing to a cablegram I received telling me of Lord Radnor's death. A year or two afterwards, I stayed at another of Lady Radnor's places on the Thames, where she imported a gondola with gondoliers, in which we went up and down the river in the afternoon, drawing much attention from the passers-by. At the age of eighty, Lady Radnor is still keenly in-

terested in everything. She even took part
in a concert only two winters ago.

For several years Lady Radnor kept her
palace on the Grand Canal and her house
in London, but having decided to estab-
lish herself in the country, she bought a
charming place at Ascot where the famous
races take place. Eton is near by, as is also
Windsor Castle. The school, the castle,
and the river make strong drawing cards.
Lady Radnor's son, the present Earl, is,
of course, in possession of Longford Castle
where I first stayed when Lord and Lady
Radnor were both still living. The English
law of primogeniture gives the eldest son
and heir the right to occupy the "throne"
or castle; therefore the widowed mother
moves on to somewhere else. Lady Radnor
moved on to Ascot.

My diary tells me that in 1901 my month
in London was largely social. I saw much
of Lady Radnor, John Sargent, and others.
Thanks to Boston associations, I was from
time to time at Mr and Mrs Joseph Cham-

HELEN, COUNTESS OF RADNOR

berlain's, informally lunching or dining with them or taking a cup of tea — once dining *formally* when all sorts of lords and ladies were there. The chief guest was the tall and handsome Duchess of Portland. Mrs Chamberlain, at the last moment, had asked me to dine. Afterwards I found that it was because I was to "fill a place." The Duke had been suddenly called away, so it was *I* who filled the place. Think of my taking the place of a duke!

I had seen a good deal of my distinguished psychological friend, Morton Prince, in London, and the two of us, in Baden-Baden, met my picturesque friend Mercer, of Danube fame, who could do anything with his hands, from building a boat to painting a portrait or making a salt-cellar. The three of us planned for a cycling trip. Mercer, dressed for the part in Tyrolean costume with a feather in his hat, never cared where he slept nor what he ate, but Prince and I were more squeamish. The Black Forest is a pleasant region but rather hilly for bicycling.

After three days of laboriously pushing ourselves uphill, we turned and slid down in an hour or two back to the spot where we had started. Having held a conference, we decided to follow the valley of the Neckar where the roads are more level. The Neckar is a lovely river with a great variety of hill and dale — hills not to climb but to look at. The little inns were sometimes fairly good and sometimes not good, but Mercer grinned and ate the food. In the course of time we left the Neckar and went to Bayreuth, our objective point. Here the various members of the Mercer family had gathered together, and had invited me to be their guest for a week. We heard *Parsifal* and *The Flying Dutchman*, each twice. One of the performances of the *Dutchman* was memorable, owing to the combination of circumstances. The orchestra and singers were performing *inside* of the theatre while a terrific thunderstorm was going on *outside*. The dramatic effect was tremendous.

After Bayreuth, I joined some friends in Munich with whom I walked and "trained" through the Bavarian Alps, a lovely country though sometimes a very rainy one. Our hotel at Partenkirchen was like an island surrounded by the floods. The only way we had of getting to and from the hotel was by boats. Later, we took a higher flight up to the Engadine, stopped at St Moritz for a week, and then went to Venice, where I stayed with Lady Radnor in her palazzo on the Grand Canal.

In 1903, while passing the time pleasantly in London, I met at dinner a friend whom I hadn't seen for a long time, Mrs Leigh, the wife of Dean Leigh of Hereford, who was a younger son of Lord Leigh of Stoneleigh. Mrs Leigh was the aunt of my friend Owen Wister and the daughter of Fanny Kemble. As I was expecting to go for a visit in Wales, Mrs Leigh said, "The easiest way to go to Wales is by way of Hereford." As nothing could be more pleasant,

I went and spent several days delightfully
at the Deanery. The Dean and Mrs Leigh
were charming, and so, I may say, was
Miss Leigh, whom I shall have occasion
to mention later. Another "cricket week"
was on, this time at Lord Chesterfield's
place (Lord Chesterfield being a descend-
ant of the "lord of manners and customs").
When we were not watching cricket, we
used to row up or down the River Wye.
Dean Leigh was a true sport, as many
English clergymen are. After the dinner
guests had disappeared, we smoked together and he told me some of his amusing experiences in London, where he had
a charge and where he was intimate with
many of the theatrical people. That was
only one of a series of pleasant visits in
Hereford. On a later occasion the Dean
took me to a performance of *Elijah* in
Gloucester Cathedral. After the first part
of the oratorio, the resident dean invited
us to luncheon with a lot of people. The
library of the Gloucester Deanery is a
splendid barrel-roofed room, the oldest

room of the sort in England, so our host told me.*

My host and hostess in Wales were Sir James and Lady Hills-Johnes of Dolaucothy, which is a fine old place of several thousand acres. The house is many centuries old. They always considered me a kinsman — Lady Hills-Johnes signing her letters "Your Distant Cousin." Since my first American ancestor came from Wales in 1692 and settled in Maryland, and as we all came from the Garden of Eden, the cousinship cannot be called near. The connection has been pleasant, however, and it has given me the chance to make several visits at the old place. At Dolaucothy there are gold mines, or caves, dating

*Going to Wales via the Severn Tunnel, which is four miles long, I feared it would be disagreeable going *under* the river for so many minutes; but to my surprise, when I asked a fellow-traveler in the carriage when we should come to the tunnel, he said, "We came through a little while ago." The moral of this is, "Don't cross your bridges before you get to them"; or rather, "Don't worry about tunnels until *after* you have passed *through* them."

back to Roman days. On the place a little museum was built, housing Roman antiquities. Among them, besides pottery, are two beautiful necklaces made of the gold from the caves. One of these my hostess wears, and the other is now at the British Museum. The mines have not been worked for centuries, owing to the expense of exploitation. Gold is, no doubt, still there; but, like Thorvaldsen's statue, it needs the dross to be removed. The little river, the Cothy, runs through the place. The oaks and rhododendrons are magnificent. George Borrow in his "Wild Wales" pleasantly describes Dolaucothy. During one of my visits, we went to Llanelly for the annual Eisteddfod, the literary and musical festival which was originally established in the seventh century. Choruses, quartets, duets, and solos were on the programme. The performances were competitive and many of them of a high order of merit. The same evening there was a performance of *Israel in Egypt* for which the chorus was composed entirely of the people of Llanelly. The Welsh are naturally musical. When we were there, Llanelly was wearing its brightest colors.

Returning to London and going to Paris, I joined Mr and Mrs Henry Cabot Lodge, staying with them for a week or two and then going on to Vevey to stay with the Theodore Dwights. The Apthorps were near by. Not far were the Paderewskis who asked us to dine with them at their château, Riond-Bossun, at Morges. Two days later I went again for a longer visit, passing the day and night. After déjeuner, Madame Paderewski said, "I will show you *my* part of the place." She then led me all about among the pheasants, ducks, rabbits, and chickens. After tea Paderewski took me up to his music room and played his new symphony and new sonata, both in manuscript. They were performed the following winter in Boston. The château was a splendid place, with a magnificent view, from the terrace, of Mont Blanc across the lake. The evening I passed there was perfect as to

103

weather. The alpine glow was at its best, like a pink rose. A number of persons were at dinner, chiefly Poles whom Paderewski had befriended. After dinner we had a little music. Before the music and just after dinner, as we were taking our coffee, Paderewski produced a bottle, saying, "As it is an extra occasion, I will give you a glass of wonderful brandy." He then showed me a tag, on which was written "1795." I can't remember by which emperor or tsar it had been presented, but I *can* remember how good it was. After breakfast, my host and hostess saw me off at the boat landing.

NINETEEN-FOUR was rather different from my usual summer. With Louis Frothingham, my legal-political friend, and R.G.F., I sailed to Holland. After spending a week there and going up the Rhine and wandering further afield, I went again to Bayreuth. It seemed to me that neither *Tannhäuser* nor *Parsifal* was so well done that year as usual. Later I spent a few delight-

PADEREWSKI AS A YOUNG MAN

ful days with Mercer and some of his relations at Aschau, near Munich, in a lovely
valley at the base of an old castle. From
there I went to Schloss Steinbach in Würt-
temberg, belonging to Baron and Baroness
von Hutten. The Baroness was beautiful
and charming, with a very good voice, so
we made music together. The Baron was a
good sort, so we went fishing. The Schloss
was a nice old place, built far back in the
centuries. The Baroness, being a mod-
ernist, afterwards decided to change her
surroundings, but she still writes novels.
None has been more successful than
"Pam."

Frothingham and I, in 1905, took the
southern trip to Genoa, stopping at Ponta
del Garda in the Azores. The little pink,
green, and blue houses of the town are
charming, spick and span, as are the
streets paved with little stones in different
patterns. It was a fête day. The inhabitants were all arrayed in gala attire, keep-
ing open house, offering cake and wine to
everybody. We stopped at Gibraltar,

landed at Genoa, and went on directly to Venice where we found it hot but lovely. After a week in Venice we planned to drive through the Dolomites, beginning our drive at Castelfranco in order to see the Giorgione "Madonna," one of the great pictures of the world. (It is a pleasure to see *one* picture in *one* church and in *one* little village and nothing else.) Asolo was our next stop, a fascinating old place with its outlook over the plain. Of course, the Browning associations here were interesting. Continuing through the Dolomites, stopping here and there for a day or two, we got our fill of beauty and color. The mountains are not always high, but the variety of color is marvelous. Finishing our drive at Toblach, we took the train and ultimately wound up in Paris, joining the Lodge family at the Hotel Brighton. After a few days, we all crossed over to London — Mr and Mrs Lodge, John Lodge, and Dr Bigelow — to the Coburg Hotel. There were many things to be done in the way of amusement, lunching and

dining, going out of town here and there.
Mr Whitelaw Reid, our ambassador at
that time, entertained royally in Dorchester House, one of the most splendid man-
sions in London with a great collection of
pictures. There was a big dinner in honor
of Mr and Mrs Lodge, with music afterwards, when Suzanne Adams and Gervase
Elwes sang. By way of adding gaiety to
the occasion, a young member of the
family, during the musical part of the en-
tertainment, fired a pistol in imitation of
certain young women of that period. The
company was so well bred that the shot
caused no excitement, though nevertheless
some surprise.

This was only one of many occasions
when Mr and Mrs Reid were hospitable.
Speaking of the splendor of Dorchester
House, Mr Ogden Mills (Mrs Reid's
brother) once jokingly said, "We live real
grand here." There was more truth than
poetry in Mr Mills's remark.

LET me now turn back to the old days in Washington and in Paris: In Washington, I always stayed with Mr and Mrs Lodge in Massachusetts-avenue. Mr Henry Adams lived in Lafayette-square. His house was given to hospitality. At twelve o'clock the round table was open every day to any of his friends who wanted to turn up for breakfast. Mrs Lodge and Mrs Donald Cameron were often there. I remember an occasion when there were men only: Mr Adams, Mr Lodge, Mr Hay, Mr Lafarge, Professor Langley, Theodore Dwight, and Charles Warren Stoddard, the author of "South Sea Idylls." After breakfast we moved over to the library, where the talk was interesting and lively. Stoddard had lived in the South Seas, a part of the time with Father Damien at Molokai, the leper colony. Stoddard afterwards showed me a cabinet filled with Damien relics. I am glad to say I never caught leprosy.

Mr Adams was devoted to his little friend Martha Cameron, the daughter of Mrs Cameron. Martha called Mr Adams

"Dobbit." Some one wanted to know what a Dobbit was. Martha replied, "Dobbit is what takes care of little girls when their mothers is busy."

I first met Mrs Cameron many years ago, when she came for a little visit with the Frank Higginsons in Boston. She had great beauty, charm, and distinction. Later on I saw much of her in Paris, where she had an apartment. At one time, when I wasn't very well, Mrs Cameron asked me to dine with her every evening, so that her cook might give me the proper food which I couldn't get at restaurants. Alas! Our paths have never crossed since. Mrs Cameron now lives in England.

In Paris, climbing up five flights (there was no elevator), I found Mr Adams in the apartment where he lived, read, wrote, and mused. Stretched out on his chaise-longue, he talked delightfully about books and people. Descending from the skies, he often dined at Larue's, Place de la Madeleine, where Mr and Mrs Lodge and I often found him in his favorite corner. At

other times we all came together for déjeuner at one or another of the restaurants
in the Champs Élysées under the trees.
That was always in the summer, when the
weather was apt to be good, as the food
always was.

At another time in Paris, Mr Adams,
Mr and Mrs Lodge, and I were together.
Mr Wayne MacVeagh happened to be
there, too, with his daughter, now Mrs
Farrer-Smith. Mr MacVeagh asked us all
to dine with him in the Bois, at the Pa-
villon d'Armenondville. Mr MacVeagh,
shirking his responsibility, contrived the
little plan of asking each of us to order a
course in turn. When my turn came (mine
was the last, as I was the youngest of the
company), Mr MacVeagh cried out, "It's
time now for the 'Joon Moossoo.'" Al-
though Mr MacVeagh had been ambassador to Italy and had filled many other
important posts, he never spoke French
well. It is needless to say, however, that
"Joon Moossoo" was an invention of his
own, made on the spur of the moment.

Forever after, I was called the Joon Moossoo. Mr MacVeagh was one of the most entertaining of men. His contagious laugh can never be forgotten. His son Charles, who is now ambassador to Japan, is an old friend of mine, as *his* son, Rogers, is.

Thanks to my intimacy with the Lodge family in Washington, I often saw Mr Roosevelt, either at his own house or at Mr Lodge's. Mr Roosevelt used to drop in at any meal — even at breakfast — when the talk was stimulating and vivid, not without its light touch. One day when we were sitting in Mr Lodge's library, Mr Roosevelt's wrath and indignation were stirred by the news of the sinking of the *Maine*. His wrath and indignation never ceased until he got what he wanted, which was the formation of the troop of Rough Riders and the triumphant victory which brought about the independence of Cuba. Mr Roosevelt certainly did more than his "bit."

Some years later, when Mr Roosevelt was inaugurated, I was invited to stay

with Mr and Mrs Lodge for the occasion.
After the impressive ceremonies, there was
a midday feast at the White House and, in
the evening, a ball. The ball took place in
a huge hall to which crowds and crowds of
people came. Mr and Mrs Lodge had a
box, from which we saw everything. Mr
Roosevelt led the procession between rows
of policemen. There was a tense feeling in
the air, many people fearing that an an-
archist might throw a bomb at Mr Roosevelt. When Mr Roosevelt had finished
with the procession, Sturgis Bigelow in
Mr Lodge's box said, "Thank God that's
over."

Let me offer my homage to the memory
of the Lodge family, which for forty years
did me the honor of allowing me to come
and go as I pleased, whether in Washington or at Nahant. The world knows of
Mr Lodge's statesmanship, but it doesn't
know of his private life, which could not
have been more charming than it was.
Mrs Lodge was a rare person, of great
beauty of face and spirit, with a wonder-

ful sense of humor. The children followed
the footsteps of the parents, adding more
and more to the gaiety of nations. Dr
Bigelow was one of the happy people belonging to the charmed circle. Others were
Mr and Mrs Roosevelt, Mr Henry Adams,
Mrs Cameron, Spring-Rice, the Winthrop
Chanlers, Mr and Mrs Douglas Robinson,
and the William Endicotts. I meant to say
more, but my memories are too sacred to
go further. Those happy days were the
brightest in my life.

AFTER these interruptions, let me continue
my story. In 1906 I took a short trip in
Spain with a painter friend. We crossed
over from Gibraltar to Tangier with its
Moorish atmosphere. The Moors are a
magnificent-looking race, tall and straight,
with dark skins to which their white tur-
bans afford a striking contrast. Owing
to Raisuli and his bandits we were not
allowed to go outside of the town, but we
saw an exciting wedding, combined with
all sorts of military manœuvres. Snake

charmers, fire eaters, and "story-tellers" were to be seen every day. In the evening, cafés and dance halls were open to the public. Tangier is more Moorish than Algiers, which has become too European- ized. Leaving Tangier after a few days, we took ship and landed at Cadiz, the whitest, cleanest-looking city I ever saw, like a pearl floating out to sea. There we heard a fairly good performance of *Trova- tore*. From Cadiz we went to Seville, spend- ing several days, seeing the wonders of the Cathedral, with the Giralda tower. We al- so saw less beautiful wonders in the way of a bullfight, when a number of bulls and horses were slaughtered for the pleasure of the populace. Traveling over to Granada, we spent a week at the Alhambra, one of the great pleasures in my life. The weather was lovely — a perfect September, which added to our joy. Later there was another joy at Madrid — seeing the pictures at the Prado, where Velasquez is at his best.

THE summer of 1908 was one of varied pleasures. I first sailed with the Lodge family, stayed a little while with them in London, then made several country visits — at Broadway, at Hereford, and at Dolaucothy. After crossing the Channel, I was for ten days at Deauville for the sake of being with some old friends and, incidentally, of meeting Jean de Reszke and hearing Clément sing at Trouville. After a little motor trip through Normandy, I went again to Mont St Michel, returning to Dives, the little inn of William the Conqueror, which has the most fascinating courtyard to be seen anywhere. I rejoined the Lodges in Paris, where we continued to do the things we had so often done, and liked to do. Once more I went to Vevey, once more returned to Paris, and finally we all sailed together for home.

Nineteen-ten brought a short trip to Ireland, through the Lakes. On Lake Killarney, we were almost wrecked, owing to a tremendous storm. Only the skill of stalwart boatmen saved us. We heard after-

wards that fourteen people were drowned
that day. Leaving the Lakes, we went to
stay at a country place in the middle of
Ireland belonging to Sir Richard Butler,
who had married Miss Leigh, the daughter
of my friends at Hereford, Dean and Mrs
Leigh. "Ballin Temple" was a nice old
place with splendid trees and still more
splendid rhododendrons. It rained in Ireland "to beat the band." My hostess never
said, "It's pouring," but, "It's streaming."
I discovered that "streaming" was the
Irish term commonly used when it rained
"cats and dogs" with some other animals
included. Nevertheless, after the deluge,
the sky was bluer than I have ever known.
Having passed several pleasant days at
Ballin Temple, I stopped for a night in
Dublin and then crossed the Irish Channel, joining five other friends for a canoe
trip down the Wye. One lovely morning,
paddling gleefully down the river, we saw
ahead of us rapids, *real* rapids, extending
for more than a mile. Having entered
them, at some distance from the start, we

came upon a drove of cattle crossing the river, and quite filling it. We had started, however, and therefore couldn't stop. How we got through without upsetting, I shall never know.

Later in that same summer, and with four of that same party of friends, I walked along the coast of Devonshire. Mr Henry White had given me a letter of introduction to Mrs Hamlyn, the chatelaine of Clovelly Court. Clovelly is one of the beauty spots of the coast. Mrs Hamlyn owned everything in and out of sight, including the celebrated "Hobby Drive." Immediately after I had presented my letter, a servant brought a note saying that Mrs Hamlyn would expect Mr Johns, with three other friends, to luncheon. As neither Mr White nor I had mentioned the fact that I was traveling with anyone else, it all sounded most hospitable. The servant, in some way or other, had noticed that I was with three other friends at the inn. Of course, we all accepted the invitation with alacrity. Be-

117

fore luncheon Mrs Hamlyn sent her carriage to bring us from the inn. Clovelly Court is a splendid house and place, with a marvelous view of the sea from the high cliffs. After luncheon, we walked and drove everywhere. After tea Mrs Hamlyn asked us to come back to dine at eight o'clock, which we did. The next day we spent the morning exploring the Hobby Drive and other places, but before we had left, a note from Mrs Hamlyn came, asking us to dine again. Not being able to resist such kindness, we once more accepted. English hospitality cannot be equalled when "the time, the place," and the rest come all together. Mrs Hamlyn liked us and we adored her, her place, and everything she did. I am sure that our pleasure was largely due to the fact that we were so well introduced by Mr White.

In 1913 Louis Frothingham and I again took the southern trip, stopping first at Madeira, where like the King of France, "we went up the hill and came down again," going up in an elevator and coming down on a toboggan. Madeira is a charming place. The plants and flowers are luxuriant and beautiful. We stayed there only for a part of a day, as we did in Algiers, a day later. The drive along the coast at Algiers is very splendid. On one side lies the Mediterranean and on the other stand the houses of the rich and great. Some of these are different embassies, as at Tangier. The Moorish quarter of the town is both interesting and picturesque. Arriving in Genoa we went directly to the Italian Lakes, traveling through them, stopping first at Cadennabia on Lake Como, at Lugano on Lake Lugano, then at Pallanza on Lake Maggiore. Going up through the Simplon tunnel we landed on the Lake of Geneva at Ouchy, where we found friends whom we wanted to see. The next move was to Paris, where we stayed for several days.

IN 1914, that fateful year when we put our heads in the lion's mouth, Frothingham and I planned to take a little trip through North Germany. This was the sixth time we had joined forces — twice at home and four times in Europe. Frothingham sailed three weeks ahead of me, and I met him at Plymouth. Thence we went on to Bremen, arriving there on July 25. My voyage was "calm and prosperous." When we got to Bremen, we had no suspicion of trouble. Reaching Brunswick, we found there seemed to be a certain unrest in the streets. This, however, didn't disturb us. We slept peacefully and the next day went about sight-seeing. The timber architecture of the houses in that part of Germany interested me immensely. In Brunswick we stayed for two days. The days were quiet, only in the evening there seemed to be more and more excitement. Hildesheim was charming. Living in a fool's paradise, we saw more architecture, particularly the cloisters of the cathedral with the "thousand-year-old rosebush," which was a remarkable sight — one root, one stem, with hundreds of branches. On arriving at Cassel, we met

the Jack Chapmans in the picture gallery.
Victor was with them. Little did he, nor
they, dream of the fate that was awaiting
him. The Cassel gallery was particularly
interesting on account of the number of
fine Rembrandts.

When we got to Eisenach, everything
was "allegro, crescendo, forte." I shall
never forget a group of young and charm-
ing-looking officers sitting around a table
in a restaurant where we were dining
near by. Such gloom was indescribable.
Not a word, not a smile, only gloom. I
am sure *they* didn't want to fight.

The next day, August 2, war was declared. It was Sunday. The whole town
was in an uproar. The church by the side
of the square was filled to overflowing.
The singing of the chorals and the solem-
nity of the congregation were most in-
spiring. We didn't know even then that
war had been declared. In fact, we hadn't
the slightest idea of what it was all about,
because we were living in the same fool's
paradise. I shall never know why we were

so blind. The thought of a real war seemed impossible; but when we got up to the Wartburg, where we expected to see everything that was to be seen, the scales fell from our eyes. We could not lunch, as we had planned, at the hotel on the hill. Not a guest, not a servant, was left. Everybody had gone. Then it was that we felt we must do something about it. At four o'clock we took the train for Berlin, where we thought we might get some real information.

Our troubles began at the Eisenach station, which was jammed. The train was still more jammed. For ten hours we sat in the corridor of the car on our valises. No food, no drink, no anything but noise and confusion. The train stopped every few minutes. Bells were clanging; guards were rushing about like madmen. The stations couldn't be seen for the trunks piled mountain-high. We arrived more dead than alive. I say "arrived," but we reached only the outskirts of the city, where, after lugging our valises for what seemed several miles, we had to make connection with the Ringbahn (circuit railway). When we finally reached the main station, the din and confusion were indescribable. It was then two in the morning, but the streets were alive with a howling mob. Motor horns were shrieking while the populace were singing patriotic songs at the top of their voices. By sheer luck, we got rooms at the Adlon Hotel, most sumptuous and most expensive. My trunk was left behind.

Coming down to breakfast, I found my old friend Mr Henry White, who had just come with Mrs White, their daughter, and her husband with two little children, from Count Seherr-Thoss's estate in Silesia. The Count, the next day, had to go under a serious operation at the hospital, but he showed great pluck under the circumstances. I hoped to get some information from Mr White about the warlike conditions, but though he had been ambassador to Italy and also to France, as well as a delegate to the Algeciras conference, he

123

knew nothing. Germany did not mean to reveal any secrets. Being uncertain how long we should have to remain in Germany, we thought we ought to husband our resources. We therefore moved to a cheaper hotel around the corner in the Behrenstrasse, which was a little quieter than the Adlon, Unter den Linden.

On the evening of August 3 we almost got into a row in a restaurant. Everybody was so excited it didn't take much to start a row. The next evening, August 4, a lot of us were dining at a beer restaurant, when it was announced that England had broken diplomatic relations. That news caused the greatest excitement. One of the ladies of our party thought we ought to leave. It was bad judgment, however, as all the diners thought we were English. Marching out in single file, we were hissed by guests and servants, which was most disagreeable. The next day we were advised by the Embassy to wear badges of the Stars and Stripes, showing our nationality. After that, we had no further difficulty. In fact, at the different restaurants we were treated with uncommon civility.

After I had made several daily visits to the baggage station my trunk was found. Let me here say a word about what used to be "German system." My trunk had been left at Eisenach. I never expected to see it again, but each day the baggage agent said I should find it in Section 30. As there were miles of sections and piles of trunks, it seemed like looking for a needle in a haystack. On the fourth day, to my great astonishment, my trunk turned up exactly where the agent said it would, in Section 30. "Mein Gott, wat system!" as the man said when he was thrown down stairs from each successive landing. The trunk problem having been solved, the next question was to get a ship to take us home and to get money enough to pay our bills. My friend, Otto von Mendelssohn-Bartholdy, the grandson of Felix Mendelssohn the composer, not only offered us money, but put *gold* into our pockets, which we returned when we found that the American Express Company would honor our cheques. After some days the Holland-America Line invented a way of putting a square peg into a round hole. So all was well, though only half well. The sequel shows that neither peg nor hole fitted.

The streets were crowded, especially Unter den Linden and Friedrichstrasse. Under our windows in the Behrenstrasse we saw, by the thousands, recruits marching to join the army, carrying paper parcels, paper boxes, handbags, every sort of thing — marching, most of them, to death. Under the excitement of war everybody was singing and cheering. These processions lasted all day and all night during the mobilization. Enthusiasm reached its highest point just after England broke diplomatic relations. "Deutschland über Alles" and "Die Wacht am Rhein" seemed to be the favorite songs. The Sunday after war was declared we went to the Dom (cathedral). The singing of that service was very beautiful. (I remember how fine

it used to be in 1883 and 1884.) The
Cathedral is a huge church; nevertheless,
it was jammed. Women fainted and had
to be carried out. After the storm and
stress of the first week, things began to
quiet down. Life became more normal.
We played about with friends from the
Embassy. Nearly every day we spent a
little time with Mr and Mrs White, com-
paring notes with them and with the Joe
Minots and Boylston Beal. Count and
Countess Moltke asked us to tea and
then to lunch. Another evening Joe Grew,
first secretary of the Embassy, invited us
to a real dinner party of eighteen — the
Minots, Beal, and others of the Embassy
— and Madame Gadski sang while Grew
played her accompaniments. It was a very
successful party and made us forget our
troubles.

One day, just before we left Berlin, we
went out to Potsdam to lunch with Mendelssohn and his wife at their charming
place on the lake. Owing to the war, everything was closed in Potsdam as well as in

Berlin. No theatre, no opera, no picture galleries. But the Thiergarten was still a constant pleasure. There we strolled under the trees and sat about. Then, too, the Zoölogical Garden was not only a pleasure but a profit. We dined there often. There the band played — the only band left in Berlin. The food and beer were good, and lots of people were making the best of the situation. To the outward view, everything was calm, in spite of the thought that brothers and sweethearts of the diners might be at the front and perhaps already dead.

On the nineteenth of August, after having passed nearly three weeks in Berlin, we took the Embassy train to Amsterdam. By courtesy, Frothingham and I were included in the Embassy car. Mr and Mrs White had with them their two little grandchildren (Countess Seherr-Thoss had been left behind to look after her husband, who had been "cut up" in the hospital). The Minots, Beal, and others of the Embassy filled the carriage. As far as the

Holland frontier we had a dining car, but after that we had nothing to eat until we got to Amsterdam excepting a bit of chocolate. The train between Berlin and Amsterdam took thirty hours, instead of the usual ten, moving at a snail's pace and stopping every few minutes, like the train between Eisenach and Berlin. At the end of our journey we were again more dead than alive. After a bath, however, and some food and comfortable rooms at the Hotel Doelen, we began to live once more.

I am ashamed to say that on the frontier my trunk was again lost. During the next ten days we stayed in Amsterdam, watching and waiting to sail on the twenty-ninth. Frothingham played golf, while I amused myself by going to the picture galleries, which are uncommonly good in Amsterdam. Haarlem, the Hague, and Scheveningen and all the outlying fishing villages, with the picturesque costumes of the natives, varied our days. As luck would have it, just as I was stepping into the cab at the Hotel Doelen to take the steamer, my trunk was chucked into the cab by the hotel porter. After that I kept my thumb on it until it was put on board the ship.

Leaving Rotterdam, we heard the cannonading in Belgium. Later in the day, passing along the English coast, we were held up by an English gunboat, which, after a while, allowed us to go. At Land's End another more importunate man-o'-war fired across our bows, forcing us to come about and detaining us for a long time. In fact, our ship was turned back in the direction of Germany. I had such a hopeless feeling I refrain from trying to describe it. Finally, when we got clear of land, we sailed a straight course for New York. I then thought our troubles were really over, but not so. After having looked about us to discover where we were going to live, we found that the square peg and the round hole devised by the Holland-America Line were *below* the steerage, right down *in* the water, not *on*

it. Luckily, Frothingham and I had a so-
called stateroom to ourselves. Most of the
other passengers were huddled together in
eights and tens. Our room had two bunks,
one stand and one washbowl, not a hook
nor anything else, but it cost a large sum.
We were called first-class passengers,
though we were in the sub-steerage. Our
only privileges were those of dining in the
first-class saloon and of having the range
of the ship. The crowd was hideous. Fif-
teen hundred passengers had to be fed in
relays, nine times a day. Fortunately, the
weather was good, and there was some
very good company — the Whites, Madame Gadski, and a number of others.
Nevertheless, like the man in the old
play, "The Black Crook," my only desire was, "I want to go home! I want to
go home!" *I* certainly wanted to go home.

HAVING been at home for nine years, I
went again to England and France in
1923 and in 1926. Both times I stayed
with Lady Radnor at Ascot, with the de

Navarros at Court Farm, Broadway, and at other interesting places. During my last visit to Paris I spent a delightful day with Edith Wharton at her charming house and gardens at St Brice-sous-Forêt, ten miles away from the city. In spite of pleasant experiences, I could not help feeling that Europe was not what it was.

Now my tale is told, for better, for worse.